Customer-Oriented Marketing Strategy

Customer-Oriented Marketing Strategy

Theory and Practice

Tevfik Dalgic
*University of Texas at Dallas,
Jindal School of Management*

and

Tulay Yeniceri
Aksaray University

Customer-Oriented Marketing Strategy: Theory and Practice

First published in 2013 by
Business Expert Press, LLC
222 East 46th Street, New York, NY 10017
www.businessexpertpress.com

ISBN-13: 978-1-60649-520-9 (paperback)

ISBN-13: 978-1-60649-521-6 (e-book)

DOI 10.4128/9781606495216

Business Expert Press Marketing Strategy collection

Collection ISSN: 2150-9654 (print)
Collection ISSN: 2150-9662 (electronic)

Cover and interior design by Exeter Premedia Services Private Ltd., Chennai, India

First edition: 2013

10 9 8 7 6 5 4 3 2 1

Printed in the United States of America.

Abstract

This book is about customer orientation as a marketing strategy. It covers the vast literature on the subject and tries to combine the major studies in this specific field of marketing and strategy to offer a comprehensive strategic tool for decision makers in organizations.

The book starts with the classic marketing concept and then reviews important developments and research of the latest findings both from the theoretical and applied points of view. Examples, methodologies, policy measures, and strategies to be implemented in order to drive customer satisfaction are the backbone of this book. Both manufacturing and service businesses are addressed.

This book also covers the relationships, applications, and steps to be taken to drive continuous relationships with customers to aid in the process of defining and implementing niche strategies, international marketing efforts, and electronic commerce.

This book is aimed at researchers, graduate students, marketing practitioners both in manufacturing and in service, chief executive officers of companies, as well as those responsible for marketing strategy.

Keywords

customer gaining, customer loyalty, customer orientation, customer retention, customer satisfaction, e-business, employee loyalty, environmental scanning, export marketing, international marketing, learning organization, market orientation, niche marketing, organization culture, organizational innovativeness, organization performance, the marketing concept

Contents

Preface

I started to teach marketing in the early years of 80s back in Dublin by using Eugene McCarthy's book. It was our textbook when I was studying management during my undergraduate years. The marketing concept was very popular and there were a general consensus among academics and practitioners that marketing concept was also refereeing to the profitability together with the meeting of the customer demand. In later years during my work in the Netherlands, I adopted Philip Kotler's book, *Marketing Management*, for my MBA classes in Henley Management College and University of Sheffield MBA programs that took place in the Netherlands.

It was 1990 when Bernard Jaworski and Ajay Kohli's ground-breaking paper appeared in the *Journal of Marketing*. I communicated with Dr. Jaworski, and I kindly asked him to send me the details of their questionnaire. He responded positively, and within a short period of time some of my students were using Jaworski and Kohli's questionnaire in their Master of Business Administration dissertations. Some of my students' findings supporting Jaworski and Kohli's model were published in articles in the local professional press in Dutch.

Later on I followed and read every piece on Marketing and tried to apply the same questionnaire in some research. In 1994 I tried to bring the market orientation concept to study and develop some prepositions for the international marketing field as a conceptual piece published in the *Advances in International Marketing*.

In 1998, I tried to explain why the Market Orientation concept was not taken up early in Europe as opposed to the USA by giving reasons in my article published in the *International Marketing Review*. In 2000 I contributed with a chapter on market orientation in *The Oxford Textbook of Marketing* edited by Keith Blois. In the same year, we published the findings of the doctoral dissertation of my student Paul Breman. In this research we found that market-oriented Dutch exporters were learning organizations, but not vice versa. The study was published in the *Advances in International Marketing*.

My colleague Tulay Yeniceri is a young marketing academic, who studied her doctorate in Istanbul University in investigating the role of store image with the store branded products' quality perception of customers. She is a hardworking, reliable, and knowledgeable person.

I think we produced an excellent source for the marketers, academics, and researchers in general.

Thank you

Professor Tevfik Dalgic
University of Texas at Dallas
Naveen Jindal School of Management

Introduction

Today the term "marketing efforts" is substantially different from that used in the past. Marketing is more sophisticated than in the past. Intensity of competition, rapid globalization, changing information technology, and changing consumer profile (socio-demographic) have a strong effect on marketing. According to the American Marketing Association, "Marketing is the activity, set of institutions, and processes for creating, communicating, delivering, and exchanging offerings that have value for customers, clients, partners, and society at large." (Approved October 2007.)

British Institute of Marketing (BIM) on the other hand gives the following definition:

"Marketing is the management process for identifying, anticipating and satisfying customer requirements profitably."

These definitions clearly indicate the following characteristics:

- Determining the needs of present and future customer, clients, partners, and society at large
- Satisfaction of these needs
- Communication
- Long-term focus
- Profitability.

Some authors argue[1] that marketing starts before the production or manufacturing by trying to identify those needs first. If there is no present or perceived customer needs—including future one—there will be no marketing. The word "market" refers to the customers, clients, partners, and society at large. Therefore, marketing is a human activity covering all human interactions, consumptions, productions, and services, from the church to the synagogue or mosque or temple. Marketing is the foundation of any business.

The concept of nonprofit marketing covers the service-related activities aiming at providing a solution to social needs, problems, and issues, and thus profitability concept changes place with the concept of increasing donors, supporters or church, synagogue, temple, or mosque goers.

Government- or public-related activities are also covered in the nonprofit marketing concept, but the aim is to provide safety, health, transportation, telecommunications, education, utility, or defense. The production or services will solve the needs, requirements, and problems of the public at large.

These basic definitions show that marketing is the backbone of any business or service or activity in any society. No matter how good your product or service is, unless it is bought or sought by the consumers, customers, clients, partners, and society at large, it means nothing. Shortly: no market, no business.

Sometimes people talk about customer satisfaction for their products or services. The issue here is how to measure customer satisfaction or, which methods to be used to measure customer satisfaction—related activities are performed by the companies, organizations, and businesses in general. Satisfying customer needs, desires, and wants is almost equal to the concept of customer orientation, sometimes called "market orientation" since market refers to human beings. In this book we used customer orientation as a synonym for market orientation.

In this book, we started with the history of the marketing concept and went through the developments, discussions, debates, and important reports as well as methodologies to give the reader a chance of seeing everything in the same publication. Additionally, some successful customer-oriented company cases are presented as samples. These cases were collected from media announcements online with sources.

CHAPTER 1

Evolution of Marketing Concept into Market Orientation

A Historical Perspective

This chapter attempts to explain the marketing concept and its progress into market orientation from a historical perspective. In order to understand the market orientation, we will review the evolution of marketing concept. In this context, the production concept, the selling concept, the marketing concept, and the societal marketing concept will be explained.

A Company Case

A Best Workplace and Most Customer Oriented Company

Mannheim, 12 April 2010—For the 6th time in a row the Mannheim Company Quintiles Commercial Germany GmbH (until January 2010 Innovex GmbH) was awarded as one of the Best Employers in Germany in the Great Place to Work benchmark competition. Practically at the same time the service company won a placement among the 50 best participants in the competition for Germany's Most Customer Oriented Service Companies." Quintiles supplies the Healthcare Industries worldwide with Clinical Research, Sales and Marketing as well as Consulting Services and Financial Concepts. Recently Quintiles with its four pillars Clinical, Commercial, Consulting and Capital has announced its new strategy under the tagline "Navigating the New Health."

(Continued)

(*Continued*)

"In a market that brings new challenges for the healthcare companies as well as for all other stakeholders a good service company must show a very high degree of flexibility, innovative power and execution skills. As in a service company everything depends on the people doing the job, only the optimum balance between customer and employee orientation can help to fulfill these requirements. The high marks that employees and customers give us in these competitions go to show that we are doing well with this balance." Monika Beintner, Managing Director of Quintiles Commercial Germany GmbH, is convinced.

For 6 years the company has been participating in the benchmark competition for Germany's Best Employers and thus belongs to just 11 companies in Germany that have been awarded so often in a row. Since 2003 the yearly benchmark exercise is conducted by the Great Place to Work Institute Germany. The Great Place to Work Institute as an independent, international Research and Consulting institute supports companies worldwide with the development of a trusting and successful working culture. A number of other Quintiles companies are Best Workplaces in their respective country competitions as well as Best European Workplaces—an accolade that Quintiles Commercial Germany GmbH attained in 2007.

Source: http://www.quintiles.com/elements/media/inthenews/press-release-gptw-dkd-englisch.pdf

In the early 1950s the marketing concept was used to explain the customer-satisfying organizations and their characteristics. This concept takes the customer at the center of all its activities, and the actions of the company take place around the customer. By doing so companies produce goods and services if they are sure that those goods or services could be sold. Otherwise, they will not be successful at the marketplace. The marketing concept in time has been closely associated with the concept of market orientation. Figure 1.1 depicts the marketing concept where the customer is at the center of all company activities and functions. Marketing/customer orientation refers to the philosophy or strategic mind-set of the organization. Some authors argue that market orientation is not a matter of

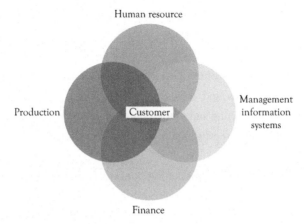

Figure 1.1. The marketing concept.

strategy, but just a methodology; however, we counter argue that market orientation changes the way a company competes in the marketplace, thus making marketing/customer orientation a strategic issue and provides that a place at the chief executive level.

In 1776 in his famous book *An Inquiry into the Nature and Causes of the Wealth of Nations*, Adam Smith, founder of the free economic system, wrote that the needs of producers should be considered only with regard to meeting the needs of consumers. While this philosophy is consistent with the marketing concept, it would not be adopted generally until nearly 200+ years later.

In order to understand market orientation, it will be very useful to overview the evaluation of marketing briefly, providing us with some important information. In early 1952, General Electric stated that their new marketing philosophy would take "the marketing man" to the beginning of the production cycle rather than to the end of it and integrate marketing into each of phase of business.[1]

Focusing on the customer has not been the hallmark of strategic planning throughout history. For example, in the early twentieth century, efficiency and quality have been the center of planning. Automobile pioneer Henry Ford has long been credited with the statement that customers could have any colored car that they wanted, as long as it was black.[2] As it can be understood from this statement, customers' needs and wants were not important for companies.

Peter Drucker stressed the importance of marketing in an organization as follows:

> Because the purpose of business is to create a customer, the business enterprise has two and only two basic functions: marketing and innovation. Marketing and innovation produce results; all the rest are costs. Marketing is the distinguishing, unique function of the business.

Keith's article[3] on the marketing concept is one of the earliest and most popular works in the marketing literature. As Keith stated in this article, American business in general—and Pillsbury in particular—is undergoing a revolution of its own today. This is called marketing revolution. The company is no longer at the center of business universe. Today the customer is at the center of business universe. In his article, Keith describes the Pillsbury Company's evolution through three managerial phases. These are called the first era (production oriented), the second era (sales oriented), and the third era (marketing oriented). At the end of these three managerial phases the companies reach a phase that he calls a *marketing control phase.*

He stated that the first era (production era) was an era when the demand for goods generally exceeded the supply. In this era, company focused on production, not marketing. He stated the philosophy of the Pillsbury Company like this: "We are professional flour millers. Blessed with a supply of the finest North American wheat, plenty of water power, and excellent milling machinery, we produce flour of the highest quality flour, and of course (and almost incidentally) we must hire salesman to sell it, just as we hire accountants to keep our books."[4] Keith states that movement from the production to the sales and later through the marketing phase has been an evolutionary process and it applies for all organizations. Keith further describes that the production and sales concepts are (as the) antecedents of the marketing concept. This framework has been widely accepted for a number of years and it has been used in several marketing textbooks. Evaluation of the marketing history is required to understand the concept of market orientation. Therefore, understanding this evolutionary process, in detail, is critical to understand the origin of the marketing concept.

Marketing management wants to design strategies that will build profitable relationships with target customers. There are five alternative concepts that will guide marketing management. These concepts are as follows:

1. The production
2. The selling
3. The marketing and
4. The societal marketing concept.[5]

These concepts will be explained briefly in the following sections.

The Production Concept

In the early twentieth century, demand for goods exceeded supply, and managers focused on efficient manufacturing and control; that is, their emphasis was on production, and the period has been called the "production era." Fullerton[6] stated that, "for more than a generation the concept of the production era dominated the understanding of the marketing's past held by students and scholars." According to him, the characteristics of the production concept are as written below:

- Firms focused their attention largely on physical production in order to overcome age-old constraints on supply with new technologies and more efficient management techniques and distribution was a secondary concern, left to independent wholesalers and retailers.
- Research regarding customer needs was less important in this era. In addition, customer needs were not crucial because demand exceeded supply and disposable income and desire for any available product grew rapidly on a continuous basis among the broad populace.
- In this era, there was little competition in each product market.
- Wholesalers and retailers did not need to develop sophisticated methods because "product sold itself" without much effort and distributors were peripheral to business enterprises,

especially retailers whose locus was manufacturing firms. Goods were scarce and customers were willing to accept virtually any goods that were available. In sum, firms did not focus on marketing in the production era.

Henry Ford, founder of the Ford Motor Company and inventor of the modern "assembly line," is sometimes held up as the archetypical production-focused executive. When it was introduced in 1908, for example, the Model T was available in a variety of colors but painting the cars became a production bottleneck, requiring up to 18 days as each of five coats was hand painted and then allowed to dry.[7] Henry Ford's managerial orientation was clear when, in 1923, he wrote that:

Salesmen always want to cater to whims instead of acquiring sufficient knowledge of their product to be able to explain to the consumer with the whim that what they have will satisfy his every requirement. He also said the following famous sentence which had been quoted by many marketers over the years:
"Any customer can have a car painted any color that he wants so long as it is black."[8]

Kotler[9] has also described the production era stating that under the production concept, managers used to believe in mass production and making productions widely available so that people can willing to buy without any marketing efforts. This production-oriented strategy predominated the market until about the start of the Great Depression in the 1930s in Western countries. The production-oriented companies are still to be found in some countries in the world.[10] In short, in the production concept, management thinks that a product can sell itself.

Product quality and improvement are important parts of most marketing strategies. As it is known, focusing only on the company's products can also led to marketing myopia. For example, some manufacturers believe that if they can, "build a better mousetrap, the world will beat a path to their doors."[11] However, customers can look for another feature to buy the mousetrap. In addition to these, a better mousetrap will not sell unless the manufacturers design, package, and prices it attractively; places it in convenient distribution channels; brings it to the attention of people who need it; convinced buyers that is a better product as concluded by Kotler and Armstrong.[12]

Businesses facing with such market and competitive conditions are often product oriented or production oriented. They focus most of their attention and resources on the other actions. Product and process engineering, finance, and production are examples for that situation. The business is primarily concerned with producing more of what it wants to make, and marketing generally plays a secondary role in formulating and implanting strategy.[13]

The Selling Concept

By the 1930s, technology had improved and effected production. In the mid-twentieth century, supply began to meet demand. In other words, manufacturer produced more goods than buyers consumed. In addition to this, competition grew. Managers recognized that promotion and selling activities facilitated sales in competitive markets. Manufacturers had to persuade their target market to buy their goods. In this era, firms focused on selling. For this reason, they hired more salespeople to persuade target market and to find new buyers. In addition to these, they focused on promotion activities. This era has been called the sales era.

Until 1930, companies had more production capabilities than ever before. After that year, the problem was not just to producing, but to beat the competition and gain customers. This led many firms to enter the sales era. The sales era is a time when a company selling because of increased competition.[14]

Keith[15] stated the philosophy of the Pillsbury Company in the following sentences: "We are a flour milling company, manufacturing a number of products for the consumer market. We must have a first-rate sales organization which can dispose of all the products we can make at a favorable price. We must back up this sales force with consumer advertising and market intelligence. We want our salesman and our dealers to have all the tools they need for moving the output of our plants to the consumer."

Many companies follow the selling concept, which holds that consumers will not buy enough of the company's product unless it undertakes a large-scale selling and effort. As Kotler and Armstrong[16] reported, the selling concept is typically practiced with unsought goods, those that customers do not normally think of buying. Insurance and blood donation are examples for this issue. These industries must be good at tracking down prospects and selling them on products benefits.

In the sales concept, conditions gradually changed from a seller's market to a buyer's market. As mentioned before, supply exceeded demand. Firms realized that aggressive selling of products resulted in increased profit. In the sales era, firms focused on selling existing products, rather than consumer wants and needs. Their philosophy was to sell what the firm produced, which was still not exactly what the consumer needed. Moreover, excessive emphasis on selling led to aggressive tactics that often offended potential consumers and backfired.[17] In the sales era, manufacturers had to inform and persuade consumers to buy what they were produced.

The fundamental problem with the sales orientation, as with the production orientation, is a lack of understanding of the needs and wants of the marketplace. As it is known, defining of customers' needs and wants are required for selling. Unless companies meet customers' needs and wants, they cannot convince customers to buy goods or services.[18]

Webster[19] on the same issue says that until the mid-1950s, the business world equated "marketing" with "selling." Under this traditional view of marketing, the key to profitability was greater sales volume, and the responsibilities of marketing were to sell what the factory had been able to produce. The focus of the firm was only the product rather than on the customer's needs and wants. The products were taken as given what the factory was currently producing, which was what the sales force had to sell. The marketing plan was short term and tactics focused only on the selling process.

In sum, according to the selling concept, consumers and businesses, if left alone, will not buy the product of the organization sufficiently. It is practiced most aggressively with unsought goods—goods that buyers do not normally think of buying such as insurance and cemetery plots and when firms with overcapacity aim to sell what they make. They do not focus on products what the market wants and needs. Marketing based on hard selling is risky. It assumes customers coaxed into buying a product will not return or bad-mouth it or complain to consumer organizations and might not even buy it again.[20]

By the middle of the twentieth century, companies focused on selling rather than on production. At this time, marketing strategies and implementations have been concentrated on persuading customers to sell products or services. In addition, promotion, advertising, and door-to-door sales have been used by companies to convince customers.

The Marketing Concept

The cornerstone of thought and practice during the mid-to-late twentieth century was the marketing concept as we stated earlier; which focused on customer satisfaction and the achievement of the companies' objectives. Having a market or customer orientation meant putting customers' needs and wants first as our Figure 1.1 depicted. At the end of this change, marketing research has been extensively used by companies. Today's twenty-first century marketing organizations move one step beyond the marketing concept to focus on long-term, value-added relationships with customers, employees, suppliers, and other partners. The focus has shifted from customer transactions to customer relationships and from competition to collaboration.[21] In a way, marketing has become managing the relationships with customers, suppliers, middlemen, and the public at large. Nowadays companies implement this strategy. Win–win approach is the basis of this strategy.

Strategic marketing consists of some critical decisions about which customers and what needs would be met by the company and by what means the company will employ to serve those needs. In other words, strategic marketing is the creation and maintenance of a market-oriented strategy, focusing the organization on the customers' needs and wants. This is the base of the "marketing concept."[22]

Many American firms have been criticized for their marketing programs since the mid-1950s. These critics have resulted in the adoption of the marketing concept.[23] The marketing concept is the basis of the modern marketing era. When an organization focuses all of its efforts on production or providing services that satisfy its customers at a profit, it is employing the marketing concept.[24] This concept has a significant importance of providing consumer value, firm's profitability, and firm's performance. Marketing concept focuses on needs and wants of target markets. The marketing concept has been redefined by General Electric Company in 1952. The landmark General Electric Company's annual report has announced a new management philosophy that stated as follows:

"[The Concept] ... introduces the marketing man at the beginning rather than at the end of the production cycle and integrates marketing into each phase of business. Thus, marketing, through its studies and research, will research for the engineer, the design and manufacturing man, what the customer wants in a given product, what price he is willing to pay, and where and when it will be wanted. Marketing will have the authority in product planning, scheduling and inventory control, as well as in sales distribution and servicing for the product."[25] This approach was new for the business world.

The foundation of the modern marketing era is the marketing concept. According to Houston, "The marketing concept is a managerial prescription relating to the attainment of an entity's goals. For certain well-defined but restrictive market conditions and for exchange determined goals which are not product related, the marketing concept is a prescription showing how an entity can achieve these goals most efficiently."[26]

Peter Drucker[27] argued marketing's role in the whole business as "There is only one valid definition of business purpose: to create a satisfied consumer. It is the customer who determines what the business is. Because it is purpose to create a customer, any business enterprise has two-basic functions: marketing and innovation …. Actually marketing is so basic that it is not just enough to have a strong sales force and to entrust marketing to it. Marketing is not only much broader than selling, it is not a specialized activity at all. It is the whole business seen from the point of view of its final result that is from the point of view."

The importance of satisfying consumer has been emphasized by Sam Walton who is the founder of Wal-Mart Corporation. He is quoted by saying, "There is only one boss. The Customer. And he can fire everybody in the company from the chairman on down, simply by spending his money somewhere else."[28]

Dibb et al. concluded that "The marketing concept is a way of thinking a management philosophy guiding an organization's overall activities affecting all the efforts of the organization, not just its marketing activities,"[29] while Carl and Gates commented as "marketing concept means that a business philosophy based on consumer orientation, goal orientation, and systems orientation."[30] They believe that firms today have adopted the marketing concept to reach organizational goals. Consumer orientation, goal orientation, and system orientation are needed to apply the marketing concept.

First, if we outline the marketing concept, consumer orientation means that firms strive to identify the group of people (or firms) most likely to buy their products and to produce a good or offer a service that will meet the demand of the target market. Second, an important component of the marketing concept is goal orientation. Goal orientation refers to a focus on the accomplishment of corporate goals; a limit set on consumer orientation. Third, another component of the marketing concept is a system orientation. A system-oriented firm creates to a system to monitor the external environment and deliver the suitable marketing mix to the target market.[31] Identifying the market segments and defining the characteristics of market segments are so important to become system-oriented firms. At this point, marketing research can be seen as an important issue to identify target market and market segment of firms. Here we again see an important requirement of strategic management, that is, environmental scanning.

Kotler and Armstrong compare the selling and marketing concepts in the following figure:[32]

As it can be seen from Figure 1.2, there are important differences between the selling concept and the marketing concept. Although the starting point of the selling concept is a factory, the marketing concept starts with a well-defined market. Consequently, the selling concept focuses on selling the existing products via sales promotion and advertising. Contrary to the selling concept, the marketing concept focuses on customer needs and integrates all the marketing activities that affect customer. As it can be understood from Figure 1.2, profits are gained by sales volume according to the selling concept. However, according to the marketing concept, profits are gained by customer satisfaction.

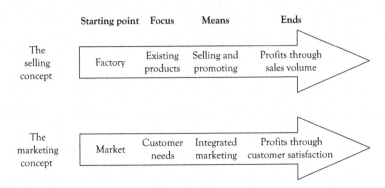

Figure 1.2. Comparison of selling and marketing concepts.
Source: Based on Kotler and Armstrong.[33]

The marketing concept is a simple and intuitively appealing philosophy that articulates market orientation. As Lamb, Hair, and McDaniel stated,[34] the marketing concept includes the following:

1. Focusing on customer wants and needs so that the organization can distinguish its product(s) from competitors offerings.
2. Integrating all the organization's activities, including production, to satisfy these wants.
3. Achieving long-term goals for the organization by satisfying customer wants and needs legally and responsibly.

The marketing concept is the idea that an organization should strive to satisfy the needs of consumers while also trying to achieve the organization goals.[35] In other words, achieving the organizational goal is also important as in the case of any strategy. The marketing concept also does not require that customers can articulate their wants, or that they even know what they will want or what will satisfy their need. The marketing concept asserts that the firms should begin strategic planning and managerial decision making with learning and focusing on customer needs.[36] Needs, wants, and demands are the core concept of marketing. As it is known, needs are the basic human needs. Human needs are states of felt deprivation. Air, food, water, clothing, and shelter are examples for the basic human needs. Belonging and affection are examples for social needs.

Knowledge and self-expression are examples for individual needs. Wants are the form human needs take as they are shaped by culture and individual personality. These needs become wants when they are directed to specific objects that might satisfy the need. Demands are wants for specific products backed by an ability to pay. Kotler and Keller have distinguished needs into five types as below:[37]

1. *Stated needs*: The customer wants an inexpensive car.
2. *Real needs*: The customer wants a car whose operating cost, not initial price, is low.
3. *Unstated needs*: The customer expects good service from the dealer.
4. *Delight needs*: The customer would like the dealer to include an onboard GPS navigation system.
5. *Secret needs*: The customer wants friends to see him or her as a savvy consumer.

As it can be understood from the above explanations, customer and customer satisfaction are the starting points of the marketing concept, defining of customers' needs, wants, and demands are required to understand a market. For this reason, we will give some brief explanations about customer needs, wants, and demands. The definition of customer needs, wants, and demand can be seen from Table 1.1.

Organizations employing the marketing concept, though must realize that any need of each consumer cannot possibly be met. If an organization tries to meet every (each) consumer's any needs, the life of organization would not be long.

Table 1.1. Needs, Motives, Wants, and Demand

Construct	Definition	Example
Need	Basic human requirements: "states of felt deprivation."	Psychological, safety, belonging, ego status or esteem (respect), self-actualization.
Felt Need	Recognized gap between current situation and desired situation.	A lonely consumer feels a need to go out and meet people.
Motive	A need that is sufficiently pressing to direct the person to seek satisfaction of the need.	
Latent Need	Unrecognized or unconscious gap between current and desired state.	A lonely consumer too busy meeting critical needs, such as food, to think about social life.
Want	Needs directed toward specific object/product that can satisfy the need: "The form human needs take as shaped by culture and individual personality."	A lonely consumer (a person who needs belonging) wants to connect with others.)
Apparent or State Want	A need–want linkage that the consumer is aware of and feels.	A lonely consumer goes to a café for its sense of community.
Unrecognized Want	A need–object relationship that has not been recognized because consumers don't understand or are unaware of the object/project.	A lonely consumer (a person who needs belonging) is unaware of online social networks that might meet that need.
Demand	Wants for specific object/product backed by an ability and willingness to pay: "Human wants that are backed by buying power."	A consumer is thirsty, wants a cola, and has the money to purchase a cola.

Source: Adapted from Mooraidan, Matzler, and Ring.[38]
Strategic Marketing, Prentice Hall Pearson, p.156.

At this point, the important question must be answered. Do marketers create needs? The answer differs from what is meant by the term need. If need is used to refer to a basic motive, marketers rarely create needs, if they can. As it is known, human motives are basically determined by human genetics and the general experiences all humans encounter as they mature.[39]

Another important question is related with the demand. Do marketers create demand? The answer is *yes* marketers do create demand. Demand is the willingness to buy a particular product or service. It is caused by a need or motive, but it is not the motive.[40] For example, advertising and sales promotion can help create demand for the products or services. It is not enough to define/mention demand that is the willingness to buy a particular product or service. In addition to this, consumers must have enough purchasing power to buy a product or services. In other words, consumers must have enough money to buy a product or services that they want to own.

According to Peter and Donnelly,[41] the aim of the marketing concept is to rivet the attention of marketing managers on serving broad classes of customer needs (customer orientation) rather than on the firm's current products (production orientation) or on devising methods to attract customers to current products (sales orientation). Therefore, the first thing is recognizing customer needs. In other words, customer needs direct the company's other tasks.

The goal of marketing concept is satisfying customer via the new products that have been produced according to customer needs and wants. With this objective in mind, marketing managers can satisfy present customers and anticipate changes in consumer needs more accurately in the future. Therefore, at the end of effective marketing efforts, customers are better satisfied and the company is more profitable.[42]

Paul and Donnelly[43] have quoted the elements of the marketing concept by King[44] stating that marketing is

1. Awareness and understanding of the importance of consumers' role in the existence and success of any firm at all managerial levels.
2. Awareness and understanding of the importance of coordination regarding the interdepartmental activities. Production, finance, accounting, personnel, and marketing departments must work together.

3. Understanding of the importance of the innovation of products and services in satisfying consumers' needs and wants at all managerial levels.

4. Awareness of the importance of new products and services to the firm's present and future profit positions at all managerial level.

5. Appreciation of the role of marketing intelligence at all managerial level.

6. Integrating all the above into a corporate strategy based on team effort to achieve departmental objectives and overall organizational goals.

Many companies have reached their aims through implementing the marketing concept. General Electric, Marriott, and Toyota's strategies are examples of successful companies that focused on implementation of the marketing concept. As mentioned earlier, market orientation is the result of implementing the marketing concept.

Lamb, Hair, and McDaniel[45] reiterated that differences between sales and market orientation are substantial. These two orientations can be compared in terms of five characteristics:

1. *The organization's focus*: In sales-oriented firms, selling of product that the company produces is important rather than what the market wants.

2. *The firm's businesses*: A sales-oriented firm defines its business or mission in terms of goods or services. However, market-oriented firm defines its business in terms of benefits its customers seek.

3. *Those to whom the product is directed*: As it is known, everybody can be customer of a sales-oriented company. However, a market-oriented company focuses only on a specific group.

4. *The firm's primary goal*: A sales-oriented organization seeks to achieve profitability through sales volume and tries to persuade potential customers to buy, even if the seller knows that the product is not suitable for the customer.

5. *Tools the organization uses to achieve its goals*: Sales-oriented organizations seek to generate sales volume through intensive promotional activities, mainly personal selling and advertising. However, market-oriented organization knows that promotion decisions are the one of marketing mix elements.

According to McCarthy and Perreault the marketing concept may seem obvious, but it is very easy to slip into a production way of thinking. Table 1.2 shows functional differences between adopters of the marketing concept and typical production-oriented managers.

Table 1.2. Differences Between the Marketing Concept and Production Orientation

Topic	The marketing concept	Production orientation
Attitudes toward customers	Customer needs determine company plans	They should be glad we exist, try to cut costs and bring out better products
Product offering	Company makes what it can sell	Company sells what it can make
Role of marketing research	To determine customer needs and how well company is satisfying them	To determine customer reaction, if used at all
Interest in innovation	Focus on locating new opportunities	Focus is on technology and cost cutting
Importance of profit	A critical objective	A residual, what's left after all costs are covered
Role of customer credit	Seen as a customer service	Seen as a necessary evil
Role of packaging	Designed for customer convenience and as a selling tool	Seen merely as protection for the product
Inventory levels	Set with customer requirements and costs in mind	Set with production requirements in mind
Transportation arrangements	Seen as a customer service	Seen as an extension of production and storage activities, with emphasis on cost minimization
Focus of advertising	Need satisfying benefits of products and services	Product features and quality, may be how products are made
Role of sales force	Help the customer to buy the product if it fits his needs, while coordinating with rest of firm—including production, inventory control, advertising, etc.	Sell to the customers don't worry about coordination with other promotion efforts or rest of the firm

Source: Adapted from McCarthy and Perreault.[46]
Basic Marketing: A Managerial Approach, Irwin, Ninth Edition, 1987, p.31.

Slater and Narver[47] investigated how competitive environment affects the strength of the market orientation–performance relationship and whether it affects the focus of the external emphasis within a market orientation—that is a greater emphasis on customer analysis relative to competitor analysis, or vice versa within a given magnitude of market orientation. Although they found no main effect for customer versus competitor focus on market performance, they did recognize that "a greater benefit might be realized from generating and acting on customer-oriented information in high-growth markets than would be provided by competitor-oriented information. Because businesses have limited resources to generate market intelligence, trade-offs between customer and competitor monitoring must necessarily be made."[48] Therefore, firms may frequently emphasize one external variable in their environmental monitoring at the expense of the other, leading to a specific market orientation profile.[49] A four-cell market orientation matrix has been proposed by Heiens. In this matrix, two important external variables like customers and competitors are combined. This matrix is shown in Figure 1.3. As it can be understood from Figure 1.3, the proposed matrix includes four distinct approaches to market orientation: "customer preoccupied," "marketing warriors," "strategically integrated," and "strategically inept."

Firms that emphasize customer-focused intelligence-gathering activities at the expense of competitor information may be classified as "customer preoccupied." Because the marketing concept promotes putting the interests

		Customer focus	
		High	Low
Competitor focus	High	Strategically Integrated	Marketing Warriors
	Low	Customer Preoccupied	Strategically Inept

Figure 1.3. Market orientation matrix.
Source: Adapted from Heiens.[50]

of customers first, many researchers consider customer focus to be the most fundamental aspect of market orientation.[51] As mentioned before, Deshpande, Farley, and Webster have stated that we see customer orientation as being a part of an overall, but much more fundamental, corporate culture.[52]

In this matrix, a company puts on competitor focus in high, customer focus in low, and this is called "marketing warriors." According to Slater and Narver creating customer value requires more than just focusing on customers. They have stated that "the key questions are which competitors, and what technologies, and whether target customers perceive them as alternate satisfiers. Superior value requires that the seller identify and understand the principal competitor's short-term strengths and weaknesses and long-term capabilities and strategies."[53]

Firms characterized as "strategically integrated" assign equal emphasis to the collection, dissemination, and use of both customer and competitor intelligence. Many researchers suggest a balance between the two perspectives is most desirable, and firms should seek to remain sufficiently flexible to shift resources between customer and competitor emphasis as market conditions change in the short run.[54]

Failure to develop a market orientation, either customer or competitor focused, may adversely affect business performance. Consequently, firms that fail to orient their strategic decision making to the market environment may appropriately be labeled as "strategically inept."[55] The external analysis is an integral part of strategic planning. According to Kohli and Jaworski, "a Market Orientation appears to provide a unifying focus for the efforts and projects of individuals and departments within the organization."[56] However, in some cases, firms may still succeed by concentrating on internal operations, technological advantages, and the establishment of core competencies. Yet, firms that fail to orient their strategic decision making to the market environment without any substantial internal strength may appropriately be labeled as "strategically inept."[57]

Toward a Responsible Marketing: The Societal Marketing Concept

"The social responsibility of any business is to increase its profits." This statement is in an essay written by Milton Friedman in 1970. Hult states that it is worth digging deeper into Friedman's article to better understand how, or not, it aligns with views that organizations today should the implement sustainable marketing operations. Hult continued in explaining his views on Friedman's statement by saying:

"In a free enterprise, private property system, a corporate executive is an employee of the owners of the business. He has direct responsibility to his employers. That responsibility is to conduct the business in accordance with their desires, which generally will be to make as much money as possible while conforming to the basic rules of the society, both those embodied in law and those embodied in ethical custom. The key point is that, in his capacity as a corporate executive, the manager is the agent of the individuals who own the corporation or establish the elementary institution, and his primary responsibility is to them."[58]

Lavidge[59] stated that the marketing people should have responsibility for serving society. According to him, these responsibilities are as follows:

- the reduction of marketing abuses and upgrading standards;
- to help in mitigating and ultimately eliminating the effects of poverty;
- to aid in improving the marketing of social and cultural services;
- to develop international marketing institutions which will contribute to improved utilization and distribution of the world's resources and, to world peace.

A new concept called "societal marketing" emerged in the 1960s. This concept deals with the needs, wants, and demands of customers: how to satisfy them by producing superior value that should satisfy the customers and promote the well-being of society. The producer should not produce products deemed hazardous to society. Kotler and Armstrong have refined the dimensions of concept. "The societal marketing concept holds that marketing strategy should deliver value to customers in a way that maintains or improves both the consumer's and society's well-being... "The societal marketing can be called sustainable marketing, socially and environmentally responsible marketing that meets the present needs of consumers and businesses while also preserving or enhancing the ability of future generations to meet their needs."[60]

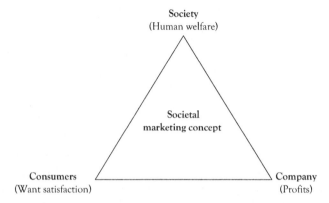

Figure 1.4. *Societal marketing concept.*
Source: Adapted from Kotler and Armstrong.[62]

The marketing concept has been extended to transcend the profit focus of business organizations to consider the needs of society as a whole. According to this broadened, or societal, marketing concept, firms must also take account of environmental, health, and safety considerations in their decision making. For example, automobile manufacturers should adapt a societal marketing concept when producing car.[61] In other words, automobile manufacturers should not only be profit-making enterprises but they should also think about environmental factors. We can observe some automobile manufacturers who have implemented these strategies. They have been focused on reducing the harmful gas emissions and some of them started to manufacture electric cars. Figure 1.4 explains this concept.

As can be seen in Figure 1.4, companies should balance among three considerations. These are society, consumers, and company. In other words, this philosophy states that an organization exists not only to meet customers' needs and wants, but also to consider the long-term effects of business activities on an individuals' or community life.

The American Marketing Association's definition of marketing recognizes the importance of a social marketing orientation by including "society at large" as one of the constituencies for which marketing seeks to provide value.[63]

Chapter Summary

In the early 1950s the marketing concept was used to explain the customer-satisfying organizations and their characteristics. This concept keeps the customer at the center of all its activities and the company's actions take place around the customer. By doing so companies produce goods and services if they are sure that those goods or services could be sold. Otherwise, they will not be successful at the market place. The marketing concept in time has been closely associated with the concept of market orientation.

Marketing management wants to design strategies that will build profitable relationships with target customers. There are five alternative concepts that will guide marketing management. These concepts are (1) the production, (2) the selling, (3) the customer-oriented marketing, and (5) the societal marketing concept.

In the early twentieth century, demand for goods exceeded supply, and managers focused on efficient manufacturing and control; that is, their emphasis was on production, and this period has been called the "production era."

By the 1930s, technology had improved and effected production. In the mid-twentieth century, supply began to meet demand. In other words, manufacturers produced more goods than buyers consumed. In addition to this, competition grew. Managers recognized that promotion and selling activities facilitated sales in competitive markets. Manufacturers had to persuade their target market to buy their goods. In this era, firms focused on selling. For this reason, they hired more salespeople to persuade target market and to find new buyers. In addition to these, they focused on promotion activities. This era has been called the "sales era."

The cornerstone of thought and practice during the mid-to-late twentieth century was the marketing concept as we stated earlier, the one which focused on customer satisfaction and the achievement of the company's objectives. Having a market or customer orientation meant putting customers' needs and wants first. At the end of this change, marketing research has been used extensively by companies. Today's twenty-first century marketing organizations move one step beyond the marketing concept to focus on long-term, value-added relationships with customers, employees, suppliers, and other stakeholder partners. The focus has shifted from customer transactions to customer relationships and from competition to collaboration. In a way, marketing has become managing the relationships with customers, suppliers, middlemen, and the public at large. Nowadays companies implement this strategy. Win–win approach is the basis of this strategy.

A new concept called "societal marketing" emerged in the 1960s. This concept deals with the needs, wants, and demands of customers: how to satisfy them by producing superior value that should satisfy the customers and promote the well-being of society. The producer should not produce products deemed hazardous to society.

CHAPTER 2

Foundations and Implications of Market Orientation as a Philosophy, Method, or Strategy

In the first chapter, we explored the evolution of marketing concept. For that reason, the production concept, the sales concept, the marketing concept, and the societal marketing concept were explained. In this second chapter, we will look at the foundations, implications, and perspectives of market orientation. Market orientation perspectives are (1) The Decision-Making Perspective, (2) The Market Intelligence Perspective, (3) The Culturally Based Behavioral Perspective, (4) The Organizational Strategy Perspective. Additionally, an important concept called "marketing myopia" will be explored.

A Company Case

Grant Instruments Wins Prestigious Best Customer Orientation Award from VWR

Cambridge, UK, May 09, 2012—VWR International Management Services GmbH & Co. KG, a global laboratory supplies and services company, has selected Grant Instruments as the recipient for Best Customer Orientation Award for 2012 at the Annual VWR European Sales Conference. Each year, this award goes to the supplier who has given dedication and outstanding support to VWR.

Ludo Chapman, Managing Director of Grant Instruments said: Receiving VWR's Best Customer Orientation Award is a tremendous honor for Grant Instruments and we would like to thank VWR for this recognition. This award is a tribute to everyone here at Grant

(Continued)

(*Continued*)

Instruments and reflects our dedication to working closely with our customers to provide the best possible customer service.

Grant Instruments was given the award for its proven first class support to VWR. By working more closely with VWR's product management team to develop the product offerings and collaborating on specific marketing campaigns, Grant Instruments helped VWR provide a better offering to its customers. In addition, Grant's customer focus was clearly demonstrated with quick and consistent responses to VWR's sales requests, participation in various customer events and exhibitions as well as by conducting a market survey throughout the European markets.

Tom Halvorsen, European Product Manager for Equipment from VWR said: At VWR, we award suppliers that have proven an outstanding ability to support VWR and our customers. Working closely with our suppliers enables VWR to provide excellent service and added value to our customers on a global level.

About Grant Instruments Grant Instruments (Cambridge) Limited (www.grantinstruments.com) is a world renowned supplier and manufacturer of scientific, life sciences, and data acquisition products. The company has been designing, manufacturing, and distributing scientific products for 60 years and has established a worldwide reputation for high quality, reliable, and robust systems designed to satisfy the most demanding applications for research in life sciences, chemical, and the general laboratory. Headquartered at Shepreth on the outskirts of Cambridge, England, the company has an extensive network of dealers and distributors servicing Europe, the Americas, and the Asia Pacific region.

Source: http://www.grantinstruments.com/company/news/grant-instruments-wins-prestigious-best-customer-orientation-award-from-vwr/

As we mentioned earlier, there seems to be opposing views whether market orientation is a philosophy, method, or strategy. In order to understand this concept let us look at some issues in the foundation and implications of market orientation.

Gaining new consumers and creating consumer loyalty are very important issues for firms in the present-day scenario due to cut-throat competition and the arrival of new companies from different parts of the world due to globalization trends.

Market orientation has a strong effect on a company's performance. To achieve high business performance, company must focus on target markets and sustain competitive advantage. Additionally, a company must distinguish itself from the competitors. At this point, market orientation can provide sustainable competitive advantage and costumer value for firms.

As a result of shift; managements' attitudes toward the markets, many organizations have embarked on formal programs to improve quality in production, enhance the responsiveness and quality of services offered, and to foster a renewed commitment to serving the customer. These activities reflect the consciousness attempts by management to develop and maintain a market orientation within the firm.[1]

Although market orientation and marketing orientation are seen by some researchers as being synonymous, there are some important differences between the two concepts. Market orientation reflects the application of marketing orientation. In other words, market orientation is an expanded form of marketing orientation.[2] The reasons for this expansion/ broadening are threefold:

1. Market orientation is not simply a concern of the marketing department, but it is organization wide;
2. The level of market orientation can avoid overemphasis on the marketing department within an organization, and can facilitate coordination and responsibility sharing between the marketing department and the other departments;
3. Market orientation means focusing attention on the market instead of just on specific customers.[3]

The marketing concept is essentially a business philosophy, and refers an ideal state or affairs. When a firm attempts to implement the marketing concept, it becomes a market-oriented firm.

According to Kobylanski and Szulc, implementation of market orientation means creation and management of marketing actions, such as environmental scanning, assessment of customer needs and expectation, and the design of goals and objectives that are based on organizational constraints, which finally lead to design of marketing strategy.[4] Strategies are designed at the top management level but the application of these strategies takes place in the market place. Any strategy should be tested in the trenches of the market place. Only the market place gives the legitimacy or acceptance or rejection of any strategy.

Schlosser and McNaughton in a lengthy study entitled "Building Competitive Advantage upon Market Orientation: Constructive Criticisms and a Strategic Solution" developed a model called "Market Orientation as a Dynamic Capability" as depicted in Figure 2.1 to illustrate how these market-oriented behaviors reconfigure information resources by supporting the views of Zollo and Winter (2002).[5,6]

They observed and reported that "the nature of strategy implies a flexible plan customized to each organization and situation. In responding to market information, employees must recognize and adapt to changing situations, and the needs of other stakeholders. Their responses change the *status quo*, and consequently, the nature of the information stored in the organization's memory."

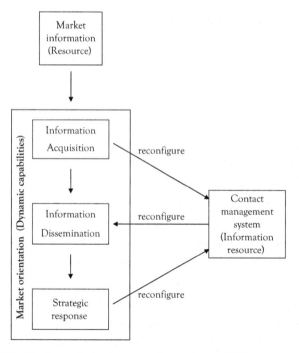

Figure 2.1. Market orientation as a dynamic capability.
Source: Adapted from Schlosser and McNaughton (2004).[7]

Finally they came to this conclusion: "This return to strategic roots increases the relevance of market orientation to practitioners as they strive to build competitive advantage. Using arguments grounded in theory, this discussion redirects the study of market orientation from a purely marketing focus to a broader strategic focus. Essentially we have explained the "why" behind previous empirical research connecting market orientation and performance. We provide a strong theoretical base supporting future empirical research into its strategic implementation."

During the beginning of 1990s, some researchers also investigated the conceptualization, progress, and measurement of market orientation.[8] Meanwhile some authors focused on market orientation to evaluate its effects on a firm's performance.[9] Several authors have given differing names or titles or groupings for market orientation.

Market orientation has been classified in different ways by several researchers. Dalgic has compiled these titles, names, and groupings.[10] The following are the most frequently used classifications:

- a corporate philosophy
- the implementation of the marketing concept
- an ideal
- a policy statement
- a corporate state of mind
- a faith
- an organizational culture
- a concept of periods or stages of development and degree of maturity of an organization that parallels the economic development of the national market within which it operates.

In addition to the given titles, names, groupings, several schools of thought have approached the market/customer orientation from their own angles and interpreted outcomes, applications, and main ideas behind this concept in their own ways. Some researchers use the term *perspective* to explain these schools of thought.[11]

Market orientation requires different perspectives and related skills, namely, thinking rationally and economically as well as understanding the behavioral issues of consumers. Johnson combined these perspectives, which is shown in Figures 2.2 and 2.3.[12]

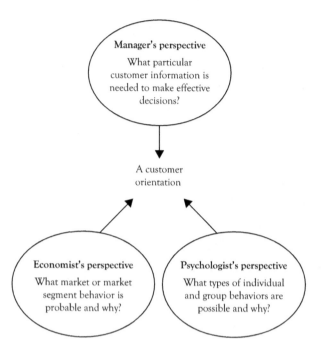

Figure 2.2. An integration of three perspectives.
Source: Based on Johnson (1998).[13]

Figure 2.3. An integration of four perspectives.

We think that in addition to those perspectives, market orientation also requires social skills from the employees of the company. We may add a fourth perspective as Sociologist's.

The Decision-Making Perspective

Shapiro suggested that three characteristics make a company market driven. These are written and explained by Shapiro as below:[14]

1. Information on all important buying influences permeates every corporate function.
2. Strategic and tactical decisions are made interfunctionally and interdivisionally.
3. Divisions and functions make well-coordinated decisions and execute them with a sense of commitment.[15]

The Market Intelligence Perspective

Kohli and Jaworski stated that market intelligence is the starting point of marketing.[16] Market orientation has been defined by Kohli, Jaworski, and Kumar "as the organization-wide generation of market intelligence pertaining to current needs of customer, dissemination of intelligence horizontally and vertically within the organization, and organization wide action or responsiveness to market intelligence."[17]

Market orientation has three components as suggested by the same authors.

1. Intelligence generation
2. Dissemination and
3. Responsiveness

Here, market intelligence is a broader concept than customers' verbalized needs and preferences that includes exogenous factors such as government regulation, competitors, and socio-demographics.

The Culturally Based Behavioral Perspective

Narver and Slater established a culture-based view of marketing. They have defined market orientation as the culture. In this view, culture and market orientation are related with each other and "a business is market-oriented when its culture is systematically and entirely committed to the continuous creation of superior customer value."[18] According to Day "a market driven culture supports the value of thorough market intelligence and the necessity of functionally coordinated actions directed at gaining a competitive advantage."[19] Day stressed the importance of developing and gathering information about customers and competitors. In other words, the market-driven business can be innovative as anticipated customers' needs. In addition to these, the market-driven business can respond to competitors' strategies and attack effectively. Here again market orientation takes the role of shaping the strategy.

There are some other researchers who have labeled market orientation as a form of culture.[20] This culture has the following characteristics:

1. It places the highest priority on the profitable creation and maintenance of superior value while considering the interests of other key stakeholders; and
2. It provides norms for behavior regarding the organizational development of and responsiveness to market orientation.

Narver and Slater have found three major components of market orientation.[21] They are as follows:

1. Customer orientation
2. Competitor focus
3. Cross-functional coordination.[22]

Webster has suggested some important requirements for developing a market-driven, customer-focused business. These requirements are as follows:[23]

- Customer-oriented values and beliefs supported by top management.
- Integration of market and customer focus into the strategic planning process.
- The development of strong marketing managers and programs.

- The creation of market-based measures of performance.
- The development of customer commitment throughout the organization.

In conclusion, as Cravens indicated "inter-functional cooperation requires getting all business functions working together to provide customer value."[24]

The Organizational Strategy Perspective

Ruekert has defined the level of market orientation in a business unit as the degree to which the business unit:[25]

1. obtains and uses information from customers;
2. develops a strategy which will meet customer needs; and
3. Implements that strategy by being responsive to customers' needs and wants.

Firstly, Ruekert has focused on the business unit in an organization (identifying market orientation in each unit of an organization) rather than the whole organization or individual market as the unit of analysis. Secondly, it emphasized strategy development and implementation in responding to the customer needs and wants.[26] Ruekert's approach has stressed the development and execution of business unit strategy as the key organizing focus of market orientation.

Ruekert has also suggested that at the business unit level, managers collect and interpret information from the external environment to serve as the foundation for selecting goals and objectives as well as allocating resources to various programs within the business unit.[27]

Lately, Lafferty and Hult after a detailed survey have identified five recent perspectives that had been added to the market orientation literature, each taking a different approach to the concept of market orientation:[28]

1. the decision-making perspective;
2. the market intelligence perspective;

3. the culturally based behavioral perspective;

4. the strategic perspective; and

5. the customer orientation perspective.

Table 2.1 summarizes the representative works in each area.

Table 2.1. List of Researchers Who Used Different Approaches to the Market Orientation

Perspective and year	Representative references
Decision-making process (1988)	Glazer (1991) Glazer and Weiss (1993) Shapiro (1988)
Market intelligence (1990)	Avlonitis and Gounaries (1997) Cadogan and Diamantopoulos (1995) Cadogan et al. (1998) Hart and Diamantopoulos (1993) Hooley et al. (1990) Jaworski and Kohli (1993) Jaworski and Kohli (1996) Kohli and Jaworski (1990) Kohli, Jaworski, and Kumar (1993) Maltz and Kohli (1996) Selnes et al. (1996)
Culturally based behaviors (1990)	Cadogan and Diamantopoulos (1995) (1990) Han, Kim, and Srivastava (1998) Narver and Slater (1990) Narver and Slater (1998) Narver, Slater, and Tietje (1998) Siguaw and Diamantopoulos (1995) Siguaw, Brown, and Widing (1994) Slater and Narver (1992) Slater and Narver (1994)
Strategic marketing focus (1992)	Day (1994) Day and Nedungadi (1994) Gatignon and Xuereb (1997) Morgan and Strong (1998) Moorman (1998) Ruekert (1992) Webster (1992)
Customer orientation (1993)	Deshpande and Farley (1998a) Deshpande and Farley (1998b) Deshpande, Farley, and Webster (1993) Siguaw, Brown, and Widing (1994)

Source: Adapted from Lafferty and Hult (2001).[29]

Marketing Myopia

The concept of "marketing myopia" was introduced by Theodore Levitt in 1960.[30] We may easily say that Levitt's marketing myopia has made a big contribution to the marketing literature. Marketing myopia is one of the essential thoughts of marketing in general and market orientation strategy in particular. As Levitt observed, "The difference between marketing and selling is more than semantic. Selling focuses on the needs of the seller; marketing on the needs of the buyer. Selling is preoccupied with the seller's need to convert his product into cash; marketing with the idea of satisfying the needs of the customer by means of the product and the whole cluster of things associated with creating, delivering, and finally consuming it."[31]

Levitt argues that the reason for the rise and fall of industries was their product, rather than consumer orientation. "The history of every dead and dying "growth" industry shows a self-deceiving cycle of bountiful expansion and undetected decay."[32] Levitt in his ground breaking article considers four conditions which guarantee this outcome. These four conditions are as follows:

1. The belief that growth is assured by an expanding and more affluent population.
2. The belief that there is no competitive substitute for the industry's major product.
3. Too much faith in mass production and in the advantages of rapidly declining unit costs as output rises.
4. Preoccupation with a product that lends itself to carefully controlled scientific experimentation, improvement, and manufacturing cost reduction.

When a company applies the marketing concept, it should first define its business. As Levitt concludes, the organization must learn to think of itself not as producing goods or services but as customers, as doing so will make people want to do business with it. An organization must avoid defining the organization's purpose too narrowly. This short-sightedness of company is called "marketing myopia." According to Levitt, an organization's survival can be threatened by marketing myopia, that is, being product oriented leads to decline, while being market oriented prevents decline.

Many sellers make the mistake of paying more attention to the specific products they offer than to the benefits and experiences produced by these products. These sellers suffer from marketing myopia. They forget that the product is only a tool to meet a customer needs.[33]

Some authors like Michael D. Richard, James A. Womack, and Arthur W. Allaway have suggested the need for a systematic way to classify the types of marketing myopia.[34] According to these authors, marketing myopia has two dimensions. These dimensions are as follows:

1. The management's definition of the firm.
2. The firm's business environment perspective.

The combination of the two dimensions produces a matrix with four scenarios. These scenarios are shown in Figure 2.4.

As it can be seen from Figure 2.4, the classic myopic firms are associated with a product definition/single-industry perspective. These firms have narrowly defined their product and so do not practice the marketing concept. This is because product philosophy often leads to the firm focusing on the product rather than on the consumer needs that must be satisfied.[36] With a single-industry perspective these firms are concerned just with the actions and reactions of current competitors. These types of firms have a single-industry perspective, that is, being concerned only

		Business environment perspective	
		Single-industry	Multi-industry
Business definition	Product	Classic myopia	Efficiency myopia
	Customer	Competitive myopia	Innovative myopia

Figure 2.4. Firm's scenarios regarding marketing myopia.
Source: Adapted from Richard, Womack, and Allaway (1992).[35]

with the actions and reactions of immediate competitors. And because of the lack of cross-fertilization of ideas they have limited strategic alternatives. In addition to these, classic myopic firms are limited in strategic alternatives because of the lack of cross-fertilization of ideas.[37]

The competitive myopic firm is similar to a compromise between the customer and competitor orientation. These types of firms are associated with a customer definition/single-industry perspective. These firms are defined by the customer needs and wants satisfied, and so they practice the marketing concept. Kotler defined "competitive myopia" as the situation wherein the management defined the range of a firm's actual and potential competitors too narrowly.[38] Competitive myopia carries the danger that a serious but latent competitive challenge will not be noticed until it is too late.[39] The competitive myopic firm and classic myopic firm are similar in terms of having a single-industry perspective and concerned only with the operations of immediate competitors.[40]

The efficienct myopic firms only partially embrace the innovative firm idea. An efficiency myopic firm partially adopts the idea of being an innovative firm. The efficiency myopic firms are defined by the product and so do not practice the marketing concept. Since they are defined by the product they do not practice marketing concept. Since they have multi-industry perspective, they do look to other industries as potential competitors and sources of solutions to problems. And their multi-industry viewpoint leads them to behave like other industries are potential competitors and solutions for their problems. Managers are cross-bred, and their experience in other industries contributes to their willingness to learn from firms in other industries. These authors stressed that these firms concerned with improvements in production efficiency, borrow only technological innovations. In other words, managers of the efficiency myopic firms focus on introducing new and improved version of existing products.[41]

As it can be understood from Figure 2.4, innovative firm is associated with a customer definition/multi-industry perspective. Similar with competitive myopic firms these firms are defined by the customer wants and needs satisfied practice the marketing concept. As stated by Richard, Womack, and Allaway, innovative firms being defined by the customer wants and needs satisfied, practice the marketing concept.[42]

In an article entitled "The New Marketing Myopia," authors N. Craig Smith, Minette E. Drumwright, and Mary C. Gentile of the French Business School Insead (http://papers.ssrn.com/sol3/papers.cfm?) suggest that a stakeholder perspective is the next step in a progression that began with "product orientation" and evolved into "market orientation."[43] Building on the insights of Theodore Levitt's concept of "marketing myopia," these authors remarked that stakeholders' orientation in marketing would help prevent companies from relying too heavily on products or services that may come under regulatory or other scrutiny actions, or fall out of step with generally accepted values. Another article in special edition of the *Journal of Public Policy & Marketing* entitled "From Market Orientation to Stakeholder Orientation," by Ferrell, Gonzalez-Padron, G. Tomas Hult, and Isabelle Maignan, has further developed the idea of Stakeholder Orientation.[44] Figure 2.5 explains this overlapping relationship.

Levitt's original "marketing myopia" concept created ideal examples of how a market orientation concept expanded possibilities for long-term

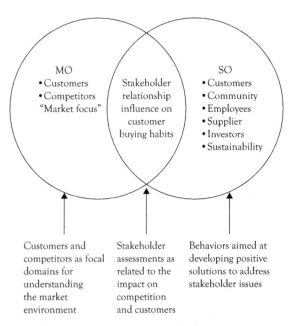

Figure 2.5. Market orientation and stakeholders orientation overlap.
Source: Based on Gonzalez-Padron, Hult, and Isabelle (2010).[45]

evolution of the companies by redrawing the boundaries of their businesses from a very narrow definition of products and services which may have a limited market for a certain time period to customer needs that could be changed or re-evaluated over a long-term period. By this way, trains were defined in terms of transportation, or black and white, silent movies have been defined in terms of entertainment or home entertainments.

These authors have suggested that stakeholders' orientation could help companies to understand, investigate, and foresee the possible developments and changes in the future market place in a proactive way. The stakeholder concept is a way of expanding holistic view and linking market orientation with the strategic management practice.

Gonzalez-Padron, Hult, and Isabelle concluded with an example that "in contrast, stakeholder orientation is a philosophy that begins with the view that the firms are concerned with the needs of a variety of stakeholders, not any specific group. This view will help prevent managerial decisions that could undermine a marketing strategy. Wal-Mart originally took a Market Orientation approach and focused on customers and competitors, but today the company has moved toward a Stakeholder approach and considers other stakeholder issues, such as employee welfare and sustainability."[46] The UK–Dutch petroleum giant Shell is another good example of taking a stakeholder's orientation into account. Because of several disasters and growing public concerns over safety, Shell had to change its strategy by paying more attention to the stakeholders' demands. Today Shell's market orientation and stakeholder orientation are treated as one single strategic practice. Wei-Skillern (2004) has a detailed work on the Shell Stakeholder experience in her article: *The Evolution of Shell's Stakeholder Approach-A Case Study*, which was published in the Business Ethics Quarterly.[47]

Although many authors prefer the word philosophy to define different orientations, due to the important roles of these "philosophies" in the development and selection application of strategic alternatives and the way a company competes in the market place we may also call them strategies.

Chapter Summary

To gain new consumers and to create consumer loyalty are very important issues for firms in the present-day scenario due to cut-throat competition and the arrival of new companies from different parts of the world due to globalization. Market orientation can provide sustainable competitive advantage and costumer value for firms.

The marketing concept is essentially a business philosophy, and refers to an ideal state or affairs. When a firm attempts to implement the marketing concept, it becomes a Market-oriented firm.

Market orientation has been classified in different ways by several researchers. Dalgic has compiled these titles, names, and groupings.[48] The following are the most frequently used classifications: a corporate philosophy, the implementation of the marketing concept, an ideal, a policy statement, a corporate state of mind, a faith, an organizational culture, a concept of periods or stages of development, and the degree of maturity of an organization that parallels the economic development of the national market within which it operates.

In addition to the given titles, names, groupings, several schools of thought have approached the market/customer orientation from their own angles and interpreted outcomes, applications, and main ideas behind this concept in their own ways. Some researchers use the term *perspective* to explain these schools of thought. These perspectives are (1) The Decision-Making Perspective, (2) The Market Intelligence Perspective, (3) The Culturally Based Behavioral Perspective, (4) The Organizational Strategy Perspective.

In order to understand the market orientation properly, marketing myopia should also be explained. The concept of marketing myopia was introduced by Theodore Levitt in the 1960s. We may easily say that Levitt's marketing myopia has made a big contribution to the marketing literature. Marketing myopia is one of the essential thoughts of marketing in general and market orientation strategy in particular.

CHAPTER 3

Market Orientation Strategy as an Application of Relationship Marketing

In the second chapter, we reviewed foundation and implications of market orientation. In this third chapter, the relationship between market orientation and relationship marketing will be explained. In this context, we will look at what is relationship marketing, database marketing, and customer relationship management.

Company Case

Kapsch BusinessCom Recognized as One of "Austria's Most Customer-Oriented Service Providers 2011"

Top service, long-term customer orientation, and the highest level of quality: these are the success factors of Kapsch BusinessCom. These characteristics are not only honored by the market, they are also confirmed in the most recent ranking of "Austria's Most Customer-Oriented Service Providers 2011," in which Kapsch numbered among the top 10. Kapsch BusinessCom was ranked among the top 10 in the cross-industry competition "Austria's Most Customer-Oriented Service Providers," making it the only Austrian business-to-business provider in the ICT industry that has earned the right to bear this sought-after seal of approval. A total of over 100 German and Austrian companies entered the competition. In Germany, the election of the best service providers took place for the sixth time, while the award was given out in Austria for the first time in 2011. The industry mix included classic service providers such as banks and telecommunications companies as well as retail and production companies.

(Continued)

(*Continued*)

"*We are proud that Kapsch performed so well in this ranking,*" said Christian Schober, Marketing Director at Kapsch BusinessCom. "*Once again we see recognition of our efforts in the area of customer satisfaction and the service quality of the 450 Kapsch technical specialists working daily with our customers. As competition intensifies in global markets, the margin for differentiation by price is thin. Only through quality and customer-oriented service is it possible to set oneself apart from other providers. We have recognized the needs of our customers, and this top showing for Austria is motivation to expand our commitment to them even further.*"

The competition "Austria's Most Customer-Oriented Service Providers" allows service providers from various industries and of various sizes to put their customer orientation to the test on the basis of a scientific model. The renowned St. Gallen University has constructed a "Seven Cs" model that evaluates the following key factors: customer orientation by management, configuration, communication, commercialization, competence, cooperation, and control. Companies are evaluated based on a comprehensive survey of customers and management with regard to these service areas. The perception of customer orientation by customers themselves is then compared with the strategic customer orientation of management.

Kapsch BusinessCom—a company of the Kapsch Group—is a leading ICT service partner in Austria, Central, and Eastern Europe with over 1,200 employees and annual sales exceeding 230 million euros. Embedded in the Kapsch Group, Kapsch BusinessCom is active worldwide with its own offices in Austria and subsidiaries in the Czech Republic, Slovakia, Hungary, Romania, and Poland. Kapsch has positioned itself as an ICT service partner offering a complete solution portfolio covering the areas of information technology as well as telecommunications. In addition to system integration and continuous optimization measures, Kapsch BusinessCom is increasingly taking on responsibility for the entire area of operations. Kapsch BusinessCom relies on manufacturer independence and partnerships with globally leading technology providers, such as Apple, Aastra, Avaya, Cisco, Google, Hitachi, HP, and Microsoft. In concert with these partners

Kapsch offers its services as a consultant, system supplier, and service provider, but above all as a reliable, dependable, long-term trusted advisor in a rapidly changing technological environment. Kapsch BusinessCom always generates clear added value for its over 17,000 customers.

Source: www.kapsch.net/en/KapschGroup/.../press_archive_2011.aspx

Globalization movement which has gained speed over the recent decades forced companies to adopt a globalist outlook through which they could enter world markets easier and compete successfully. As Manu observed "growth in the internationalization of business and markets has led to a greater need for analysis of the role and the effectiveness of strategies in different geographic markets. Such an analysis requires an examination of whether particular strategies are associated with particular market characteristics and with particular kinds and levels of business performance."[1] This local market adaptation approach requires some organizational change and strategy development suitable to those markets; this is due to the inherent cultural, socio-political, and environmental differences that already exist in national markets. This approach takes us to the Scandinavian view point of Relationship Marketing as suggested by Grönroos (1994).

He concluded that the paradigm had changed in marketing management and marketing requires a new perspective, which is more market-oriented and less manipulative and where the customer indeed is the focal point as suggested by the marketing concept.[2] The same author in his analysis of marketing history and practice observes that due to the practice of marketing mix, namely product, price, place, and promotion, "Marketing department is separated from other activities of the firm and delegated to specialists who take care of the analysis, planning, and implementation of various marketing tasks, such as market analysis, marketing planning, advertising, sales promotion, sales, pricing, distribution, and product packaging. However, the organizational approach inherent in the marketing mix management paradigm is not very useful." Grönroos further observed that Piercy Webster have reached similar conclusions.[3]

Figure 3.1 represents the comparison of 4P-based marketing approach and what Grönroos calls "relationship-based" marketing strategies.[4]

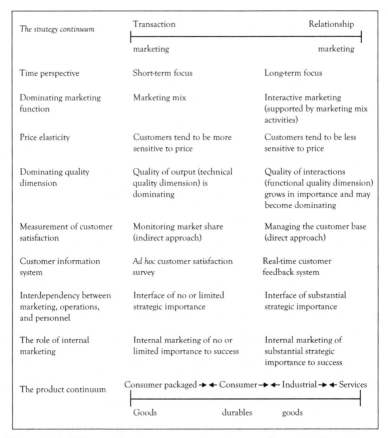

The strategy continuum	Transaction marketing	Relationship marketing
Time perspective	Short-term focus	Long-term focus
Dominating marketing function	Marketing mix	Interactive marketing (supported by marketing mix activities)
Price elasticity	Customers tend to be more sensitive to price	Customers tend to be less sensitive to price
Dominating quality dimension	Quality of output (technical quality dimension) is dominating	Quality of interactions (functional quality dimension) grows in importance and may become dominating
Measurement of customer satisfaction	Monitoring market share (indirect approach)	Managing the customer base (direct approach)
Customer information system	*Ad hoc* customer satisfaction survey	Real-time customer feedback system
Interdependency between marketing, operations, and personnel	Interface of no or limited strategic importance	Interface of substantial strategic importance
The role of internal marketing	Internal marketing of no or limited importance to success	Internal marketing of substantial strategic importance to success
The product continuum	Consumer packaged →← Consumer →← Industrial →← Services Goods durables goods	

Figure 3.1. The marketing strategy continuum: Some implications.
Source: Based on Grönroos Christian (1997).[5]

In the same token as Sheth, Gardner, and Garrett observed "… we need to expand our understanding of marketing to incorporate the basic tenets of marketing, that is, market behavior market transactions as the unit of analysis, marketing as a dynamic process of relationships between buyers and sellers, and the exogenous variables that influence market behavior … What is needed is a perspective that reflects the *raison d'être* (reason of existence) of marketing, a perspective that is the common cause that no stakeholder (consumer, seller, government, or social critic) can question. Indeed that perspective should really reflect what marketing is all about."[6]

Although Grönroos attempted to distinguish between market orientation and relationship marketing orientation, many authors did not make this distinction.[7] In our opinion, market orientation includes a relationship with its customers, stakeholders, and its environmental forces in general. Instead of using a separate market orientation/customer orientation terminology we may use the generally accepted term relationship marketing. Berry coined the term relationship marketing and defined it as "attracting, maintaining, and enhancing customer relationships."[8] This term has gained a widespread recognition among scholars and marketing practitioners. Harker reviewed 26 definitions of relationship marketing, and suggested the following new and comprehensive definition: "An organization engaged in proactively creating, developing, and maintaining committed, interactive, and profitable exchanges with selected customers (partners) over time is engaged in relationship marketing." By using this definition we may also link the marketing functions with the overall management of the company and its other business activities as a part of the corporate strategy.[9]

This takes us to the concept of business relationship management as Sin et al. concluded that "a strategy employed by an organization in which a continuous level of engagement is maintained between the organization and its audience.[10] Relationship management can be between a business and its customers (customer relationship management) and between a business and other businesses (business relationship management). Relationship management is a focus of the financial and investing industries as a way to identify potential cross-sales of products and services."

Later on this term has become more popular when the focus of marketers started to switch from customer acquisition to customer retention. In our opinion the whole process of marketing strategy has become a relationship management with the customers, stakeholders, and the public and environment at large. In this highly technologically moderated and information-based society, customers have become very sophisticated and demanding; and their loyalties have been losing ground to products themselves and as a conclusion this relationship management strategy model seems to be more appropriate. This strategic approach links relationship marketing with niche marketing practices where the customer is the center of all corporate activities. Some important data about customer retention as follows:[11]

- Acquiring new customers can cost five times more than satisfying and retaining current ones. It requires a great deal of effort to induce satisfied customers to switch from their suppliers.
- The average company loses 10 percent of its customers each year.
- A 5 percent reduction in the customer defection rate can increase profits by 25 percent to 85 percent, depending on the industry.
- Profit rate tends to increase over the life of the retained customer due to increased purchases, referrals, price premiums, and reduced operating costs to service.

A US researcher McKenna (1991) defined the relationship marketing as "involving the application of the marketing philosophy to all parts of the organization" and he defines every employee as a "part-time marketer." The same author in his famous Harvard Business Review article used the title *Marketing is everything* and he proposed that six principles are at the heart of marketing.[12] These principles can be outlines in the following sequence:

1. "Marketing is everything and everything is marketing," suggests that marketing is like quality. It is not a function but an all-pervasive way of doing business.
2. "The goal of marketing is to own the market, not just to sell the product," is a remedy for companies that adopt a limiting "market-share mentality." When you own a market, you lead the market.
3. "Marketing evolves as technology evolves." Programmable technology means that companies can promise customers "anything, any way, any time." Now marketing is evolving to deliver on that promise.
4. "Marketing moves from monologue to dialogue," argues that advertising is obsolete. Talking at customers is no longer useful. The new marketing requires a feedback loop—a dialogue between company and customer.
5. "Marketing a product is marketing a service is marketing a product." The line between the categories is fast eroding: the best manufacturing

companies provide great service, the best service companies think of themselves as offering high-quality products.

6. "Technology markets technology," points out the inevitable marriage of marketing and technology and predicts the emergence of marketing workstations, a marketing counterpart to engineers' CAD/CAM systems.

In our research we have found that relationship marketing is different from other forms of marketing and it gives great importance to the long-term value of customer relationships and extends the communications beyond the advertising and other sales promotion methods and practices.

A German author named Büschke claimed that customer satisfaction concept is a trap.[13] He dismisses much of customer satisfaction as "a trap," and places customer switching costs at the heart of loyalty. If the costs of switching products exceed the benefits, customers will remain loyal, at least in a behavioral sense. They are "locked-in." The notion of a lock-in is risky because many marketers who think their customers are locked-in actually are on the brink of an arrogance-induced loss of customers who resent being taken for granted or treated like captives. Another group of researchers Keiningham Vavra, Aksoy and Wallard et al. (2005) in their book concluded that the history of exploration into customer loyalty has been "long, if not enlightening."[14] They cited a review that found more than 50 different operational definitions of "loyalty," while some of the book's 53 myths are "straw men," unlikely to surprise most marketers, others are not only counterintuitive, but also run counter to what you are likely to read in loyalty books written by people who do no research. For example, Myth 42 is "Loyal customers are less price sensitive." And Myth 44 is "Loyal customers are more profitable." They found that the support for some myths is stronger than for others.[15] The motivation for "locked-in" strategy is to keep control of the relationship and, in doing so, exercise indirect control over potential competitors by keeping them out of a particular market.[16] "Locking-in" customers could have a negative connotation in that customers may be in a relationship against their will, particularly in the latter stages of the relationship. Researchers Schlesinger and Heskett have created a new dimension to the loyalty issue by bringing in a new concept to the picture by a label "employee loyalty."[17]

They created the "cycle of success" and "cycle of failure" for employees in relation to the issues of customer loyalty and satisfaction. "In the cycle of success, an investment in your employees' ability to provide superior service to customers can be seen as a virtuous circle. Effort spent in selecting and training employees and creating a corporate culture in which they are empowered can lead to increased employee satisfaction and employee competence."[18]

Reichheld, another researcher, has expanded the loyalty concept further by adding loyalty of suppliers, employees, bankers, customers, distributors, shareholders, and the board of directors.[19]

The weakness of "locked-in" concept brings us to a conclusion: How we can keep the customers, if "locked-in" and "loyalty" are not enough to keep them as our customers? The answer here is to create relationships with the customers and keep control these relationships with the existing customers that require a new strategy; it is called customer retention strategy. This strategy aims at keeping the existing customers continue to do business with the company, while customer "regain" strategy aims at regaining the customers who left the company. For the future customers or potential customers, the strategy to be employed is customer "gain" strategy as in a matrix developed by Dalgic.[20]

Figure 3.2 explains the types of customers and the required customer relationship strategies.

Customer type	Customer relationship strategy
Past	Regain
Existing	Retain
Potential	Gain

Figure 3.2. Matrix of customer types and customer relationship strategies.

Companies in order to apply customer retention strategy may develop several techniques, one of them being the database marketing approach. Copulsky and Wolf suggest that the establishment of a database of current and potential customers enables organizations to deliver a differentiated message to these customers based on their characteristics and preferences and to monitor the cost of acquiring customers and their lifetime value to the organization.[21] Strategy researchers Treacy and Wiersema suggest that a strategy of using information technology to maintain detailed information on customers allows marketers to differentiate and to direct marketing programs to customers on an individualized basis.[22] By doing so, companies may know their customers intimately and will be able to target them more effectively by providing right products and services with right marketing mix tools.

There is also another concept called customer relationship management which is an implemented strategy for managing a company's interactions with customers, clients, and sales prospects. It involves using technology to organize, automate, and synchronize business processes—principally sales activities, but also those for marketing, customer service, and technical support.[23]

In the services marketing Parasuraman, Zeithaml, and Berry developed a model to measure customer satisfaction called Servqual-Service Quality."[24] This model provides the fundamental issues in the measurement of customer satisfaction with a service activity by using "gap analysis" between the customer's expectation of performance and the service providers' own perceived experience of performance.

Chapter Summary

Globalization movement which has gained speed over the recent decades forced companies to adopt a globalist outlook through which they could enter world markets easier and compete successfully. Paradigm changed in marketing management. Grönroos (1994) has concluded that marketing requires a new perspective, which is more market oriented and less manipulative and where the customer indeed is the focal point as practiced by the marketing concept.[25]

In our research we have found that relationship marketing is different from other forms of marketing and it gives great importance to the long-term value of customer relationships and extends the communications beyond the advertising and other sales promotion methods and practices.

Although Grönroos attempted to distinguish between market orientation and relationship marketing orientation, many authors did not make this distinction. In our opinion, market orientation includes a relationship with its customers, stakeholders, and its environmental forces in general. Instead of using a separate market orientation/customer orientation terminology we may use the generally accepted term relationship marketing. We may also link the marketing functions with the overall management of the company and its other business activities as a part of the corporate strategy.

The weakness of "locked-in" concept brings us to a conclusion: How we can keep the customers, if "locked-in" and "loyalty" are not enough to keep them as our customers? The answer here is to create relationships with the customers and keep control of these relationships with the existing customers that require a new strategy. This is called customer retention strategy. This strategy aims at keeping the existing customers continue to do business with the company, while customer "regain" strategy aims at regaining the customers who left the company. For the future customers or potential customers the strategy to be employed is customer "gain" strategy as in a matrix developed by Dalgic.[26]

CHAPTER 4

How to Become a Market-Oriented Organization

In the previous chapter, we examined the relationship between market orientation for the new companies from the normative point of view by using previous research and lessons derived from the market examples. In this chapter, we will also look at how to become a market-oriented organization. Additionally, the traditional and market-oriented organizational structures will be compared.

A Company Case

FedEx Ranks Number One in Customer Satisfaction Among Express Delivery Companies For 12th Consecutive Year

MEMPHIS, Tenn., June 08, 2009—FedEx Corp. (NYSE: FDX) today ranked number one in customer satisfaction in Express Delivery industry and also the first among 81 companies whose customers are surveyed in the first quarter by the University of Michigan's American Customer Satisfaction Index (ACSI). "At FedEx, we believe there is a crucial link between team members' satisfaction and customer satisfaction and loyalty," said Cary Pappas, president of FedEx Customer Information Services. "The high ranking in the ACSI is a testament to all the outstanding FedEx team members who are committed to making every FedEx experience outstanding."

FedEx has ranked number one in the Express Delivery industry for 12 consecutive years. In the first quarter of the year, ACSI measures customer satisfaction with the quality of products and services in

(Continued)

(Continued)

utilities, transportation and warehousing, information, health care and social assistance, and accommodation and food services.

The ACSI is the only national, cross-industry measure of the quality of U.S. economic output and scores companies based on customer expectations, quality, value and intention to re-purchase.

About the American Customer Satisfaction Index (ACSI)

The American Customer Satisfaction Index is a national economic indicator of customer evaluations of the quality of products and services available to household consumers in the United States. It is updated each quarter with new measures for different sectors of the economy replacing data from the prior year. The overall ACSI score for a given quarter factors in scores from about 200 companies in 44 industries and from government agencies over the previous four quarters. The Index is produced by the University of Michigan's Ross School of Business in partnership with the American Society for Quality and CFI Group.

About FedEx Corp.

FedEx Corp. (NYSE: FDX) provides customers and businesses worldwide with a broad portfolio of transportation, e-commerce and business services. With annual revenues of $38 billion, the company offers integrated business applications through operating companies competing collectively and managed collaboratively, under the respected FedEx brand. Consistently ranked among the world's most admired and trusted employers, FedEx inspires its more than 290,000 team members to remain "absolutely, positively" focused on safety, the highest ethical and professional standards and the needs of their customers and communities. For more information, visit news.fedex.com.

Source: http://news.van.fedex.com/ACSI2009

We believe that market orientation and its application in the marketplace may show a difference between an entirely new company and an existing company to increase its market orientation. For the new company the requirements are easy to apply, but for an existing company it requires an implant, which may take patience, time, and change in the organization culture as well as in training the personnel and several attempts to alter the ways the company did business.

Marketing literature has a very rich collection of works and studies accumulated on market orientation over more than 50 years, the application side of how to become a market-oriented organization has not been answered in one single method. Studies of Day, Felton, King, and Barksdale and Darden are some of the literature works.[1] In the previous chapter we have outlined several schools of thought or approaches; here we will concentrate on the practical part of market orientation by reviewing the literature.

The concept of market orientation has been seen as "a cornerstone of both strategic marketing and strategic management."[2] Supporting entire workforce is required to become market oriented. Executives have an important role in the process. Executives must identify changing customer needs and wants and determine the impact of these changes on the consumer satisfaction. In addition to these, executives must increase the rate of product/service innovation in business strategies, and develop strategies that provide competitive advantages to the firm.[3] For these reasons, we can say that the role of executives is too important to become a market-oriented firm. Executives must encourage employees to understand consumer needs, wants, and demand. As it is mentioned earlier, consumer is the main point of business implementation in a market-oriented organization.

Some authors classified the capabilities of market-driven organizations. For example, Day for example approached the issue from strategic point of view.[4] Day suggested that the strategic importance of capabilities lies in their demonstrable contribution to sustainable competitive advantages and superior profitability.

According to him, it is not possible to enumerate all possible capabilities,[5] because every business develops its own configuration of capabilities that is rooted in the realities of its competitive market, past commitments, and anticipated requirements. Day has classified the capabilities of market-driven organizations in Figure 4.1.

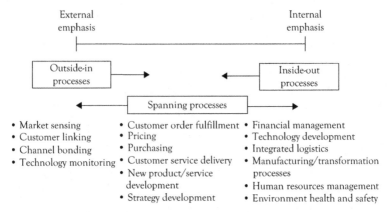

Figure 4.1. Classifying capabilities of market-driven companies.
Source: Adapted from Day.[6]

As Figure 4.1 explains, the stated capabilities of market-driven organizations can be classified into three groups depending on the orientation and focus of the defining processes. At the end of the spectrum are those that are deployed from the inside out and activated by market requirements, competitive challenges, and external opportunities. Manufacturing and other transformation activities, logistics, and human resource management, including recruiting, training, and motivating employees can be given examples. As Day observed, at the end of the spectrum are those capabilities whose focal point is almost exclusively outside the organization.[7] The purpose of these outside-in capabilities is to connect the processes that define the other organizational capabilities to the external environment and enable the business to compete by anticipating market requirements ahead of competitors and creating durable relationships with customers, channel members, and suppliers. As it can be seen before Figure 4.1, the function of spanning capabilities is to integrate the inside-out and outside-in capabilities. Customer order fulfillment, pricing, purchasing, customer service delivery, new product/service development, and strategy development are critical activities that must be informed by both external and internal analyses.[8]

Webster on the other hand stated that companies subscribing to the new marketing concept will not have a central marketing department that reviews and approves all activities involving the company's product offering and relationship with the customers.[9] In addition to this,

Webster stressed that marketing's job under the new marketing concept is to provide information to decision makers throughout the organization and develop total marketing programs, thus making the management a market-driven management. Webster has suggested 15 guidelines for the market-driven manager. They are as follows:

1. Create customer focus throughout the business
2. Listen to the customer
3. Define and nurture your distinctive competence
4. Define marketing as marketing intelligence
5. Target customers precisely
6. Manage for profitability, not sales volume
7. Make customer value the guiding star
8. Let the customer define quality
9. Measure and manage customer expectations
10. Build customer relationships and loyalty
11. Define the business as a service business
12. Commit to continuous improvement and innovation
13. Manage culture along with strategy and structure
14. Grow with partners and alliances
15. Destroy marketing bureaucracy.

These guidelines and the views of other researchers can be outlined as below:

Create Customer Focus Throughout the Business

From top management to down, people throughout the entire organization must focus on creating customer satisfaction. The customer must be put on a pedestal, standing above all others in the organization, including the owners and the managers. The CEO must be the chief advocate for the customer, frequently stating the primacy of customer satisfaction as a goal of the business and making the tough decisions when necessary to show everyone else in the organization that the customer always the first.[10] In other words, the CEO must encourage all people in the organization to adopt customer orientation.

Listen to the Customer

The customer-oriented company must be sensitive to its customers and thus it listens to its customers as individuals and understands their perceptions, expectations, needs, and wants. Especially, customer complaints about products, services, and people who work in that company must be listened to carefully. Customer complaints must be attended to immediately because the negative word of mouth has a negative impact on potential customers.

Other opportunities for listening to the customer occur on every sales and service call, every time the customer calls in an order, and every time someone inquires about an order, a delivery or an invoice.[11] Other authors have also supported this view. Market-oriented companies develop an in-depth understanding of their customer base as well as actions of competitors and often attempt to satisfy these desires through innovative product or services.[12]

Define and Nurture Your Distinctive Competence

Webster states that the old mass marketing concept lacked strategic impact because it did not consider the difficult task of matching up customer needs with the firm's capabilities. It never really addressed the question of which customer and which needs the company should focus on, expect the relatively unsatisfied ones.[13]

Define Marketing as Marketing Intelligence

Customer knowledge is an important value for a company. A market-driven company must have knowledge about current and potential customers. Webster has also stressed the importance of market intelligence. "In the market-driven company, every important judgment manager make must be based on current, complete, and correct information about the market, including assessment of both customers and competitors. Part of the customer-knowledge competence of an organization is the sophisticated understanding of customers and their needs that resides in the minds of management and other decision makers. The other part and another key strategic resource is the company's customer database."[14]

Target Customers Precisely

The essence of being market driven is to know which customers belong to us and which belong to our competitors. Market segmentation, targeting, and positioning still are the critical strategic choices under the new marketing concept. A market-oriented company should select customers carefully based on major segmentation variables. Geographic, demographic, psychographic, benefit, and usage rate segmentation may be used for segmenting the customers. Researchers, Kotler and Keller classified the main characteristics of a segment as follows:[15]

- *Measurable*: The size, purchasing power, and characteristics of market can be measured.
- *Substantial*: The market segments must have enough size and be profitable that can be serving.
- *Accessible*: The market segments can be accessible by the company. In other words, the market segments can be reached effectively.
- *Differentiable*: The segments are conceptually distinguishable and respond differently to different marketing mix components.
- *Actionable*: Effective programs can be formulated for attracting and serving the segments.

Manage for Profitability, not Sales Volume

As stated by Webster, the strategic importance of targeting lies in the assumption that the firm should be managed for profitability, not sales volume. Profit is a measure of the value firm has created for the customer and an indicator of how well the company has understood customer needs and translated that understanding into products and services that deliver superior value.[16] Especially, a market-driven company must be attentive to make price decision.

Make Customer Value the Guiding Star

Managers can use market intelligence to make sure everyone in the company understands how the customer defines value and how that definition evolves over time. Customer orientation and market information combine to create a functioning organizational commitment to delivering superior value. As it is known, delivering superior value to customers should be a part of the organization culture. Delivering superior value to customers should be put in the company's mission statement.[17]

Strategies that emphasize creating customer value all depend on building distinctive market sensing and customer-linking capabilities and using these capabilities to guide the internal processes.[18]

Treacy and Wiersema have emphasized three distinct ways to create customer value.[19] These are as follows:

1. *Operational excellence*: Trough price and convenience leadership requires business processes that minimize overhead and internal transaction costs and manage close links to customers and channel partners.

2. *Customer intimacy*: Strategies emphasize the ability to continuously tailor products and services to increasingly fine customer definitions; a highly developed market-sensing capability is essential so that shifting requirements can be identified as early as possible.

3. *Product leadership*: This is attained with a continuous stream of innovative products and services. Here again, a market-sensing capability—recognizing emerging needs, rapidly assessing customer response, and designing rapid market entry strategies—is a key contributor to the success of this strategy.

Let the Customer Define Quality

In general, quality, value, and customer orientation are all the same thing. According to Webster, to put the concept into operation, quality must be translated into specific product performance characteristics that contribute to customer satisfaction and be measured. The new marketing concept uses customer expectations as the benchmark.

Total quality management (TQM) concept on the other hand supports Webster's views. TQM is the commitment by all departments to the strategic goal of achieving quality. Total quality management does not, however, equate to comparing an end product to an approved standard. TQM in its basic philosophy draws a parallel to the new marketing concept. However, quality management is not the same as quality control.[20] As Garvin stressed,[21] all definitions of TQM are anchored in the concept of customer satisfaction; the customer is the ultimate arbiter of quality. Schonberger[22] defines TQM as "a set of concepts and tools for getting all employees focused on continuous improvement, in the eyes of customer-the next process as well as the final consumer" and shows a parallel thinking to the Webster's.

Measure and Manage Customer Expectations

Market-oriented approach consists of learning about market and using it for marketing strategy and implementations. Market orientation pays attention not only to customers, but also to many of factors effective of needs, decisions, and preferences of customers.[23]

Customer satisfaction is typically defined as the degree to which a product meets or exceeds the customer's expectations about the product. The key point in this definition is the understanding of customer expectations and how they are formed. Expectation level is related to alternatives that customer has. In other words, if customers have many alternatives for meeting their needs, their expectations will be higher.[24] We can say that customer expectation depends on some factors.

According to Webster,[25] managing customer expectations may have both positive and negative consequences. On the negative side, marketers must beware of "overpromising" when making product performance claims. If marketers segment and target their markets carefully, they will not face this type of problem. On the positive side, marketing communications of all kinds represent an opportunity to inform and educate the customer and create expectations against which the company wishes to be judged and compared with its competitors. If your company's product offers superior value, selling messages can promise customers that they can increase their expectations and still have them satisfied.[26]

Build Customer Relationships and Loyalty

As we covered in detail before, loyalty refers to a strong commitment to repurchase a superior product or service in future so that the same brand or product will be purchased despite marketing efforts by potential rivals.[27]

Satisfied customers are the company's customer relationship capital. If the company is sold, the acquiring company would pay not only for the plant and equipment and brand name, but also for the delivered customer base, the number and value of customers who will do business with the new firm.

According to Kotler and Keller, winning companies improve that value by excelling at strategies like the following:[28]

- *Reducing the rate of customer defection*: A market-driven company can reduce the rate of customer defection by selecting and training employees to be knowledgeable and friendly.
- *Increasing the longevity of the customer relationship*: The more engaged with the company, the more likely a customer is to stick around.
- Enhancing the growth potential of each customer through "share of wallet," cross selling, and up selling. Sales from existing customers can be increased with new offerings and opportunities. Harley-Davidson sells more than motorcycles and accessories like gloves, leather jackets, helmets, and sun-glasses. A present-day example for this situation would be Apple.
- *Making low-profit customers more profitable or terminating them*: To avoid the direct need for termination, marketers can encourage unprofitable customers to buy more or in larger quantities, or pay higher amounts or fees.
- *Focusing disproportionate effort on high-profit customers*: The most profitable customers can be treated in a special way. Thoughtful gestures such as birthday greetings, small gifts, or invitations to special sports events can send them a strong positive signal.

Define the Business as a Service Business

Defining the products as a service leads to defining the business as a service business. Because the service bundle can differentiate your products from those of the competitors, value delivery processes need continuous monitoring, improvement, and reengineering as much as product does.[29]

Commit to Continuous Improvement and Innovation

A market-driven organization must focus on continuous improvement and innovation. Companies have no alternatives apart from innovation and improvement. As it is known, organizations operate in global and intense competitive environment. Innovation and improvement are related to "newness" concept.

What does new mean for new product marketing? Newness is classified into four points of view by Kerin, Hartley, and Rudelius.[30] These are as follows:

1. newness compared with existing products;
2. newness in legal terms;
3. newness from the organization's perspective;
4. newness from consumer's perspective.

The last way to define new products is in terms of their effects on consumption. This approach can be seen from Figure 4.2.

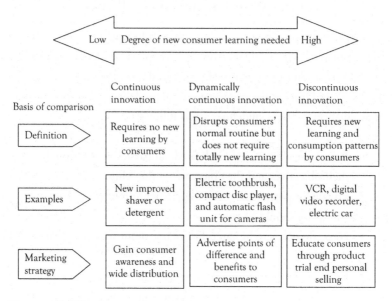

Figure 4.2. The degree of newness.

Source: Adapted from Kerin, Hartley, and Rudelius.[31]

As it can be seen from Figure 4.2, the degree of newness in a new product affects the amount of learning effort consumers must exert to use the product and the resulting marketing strategy.[32]

As stated by Kerin, Hartley, and Rudelius, successful organizations view newness and innovation in their products at three levels. At the lowest level, which usually involves the least risk, is a product line extension. Product line extension is an incremental improvement of existing product for the company. At the next level is a significant jump in the innovation or technology, such as from a desktop computer to a laptop. The third level is true innovation, a truly revolutionary new product, such as the first Apple computer in 1976.

Manage Culture Along With Strategy and Structure

A market-driven organization must manage organizational culture because managing organizational culture is very important. This subject will be covered in detail later.

Grow With Partners and Alliances

Changing environmental conditions cause different organization design requirements. Strategic alliance is one of the organizational changes. The rate of formation of international strategic alliances has been raised after 1990s. Peter Drucker has proposed several guidelines for improving strategic alliances.[33] These guidelines are as follows:

- Before the alliance is complicated, all parties must through their objectives and the objectives of the "child."
- Equally important is advance agreement on how the joint enterprise should be run.
- Next, there has to be careful thinking about who will manage the alliance.
- Each partner needs to make provision in its own structure for the relationship to the joint enterprise and the other partners.
- Finally, there has to be prior agreement on how to resolve disagreement.

Destroy Marketing Bureaucracy

Marketing bureaucracy has been part of the problem in the past; and it is clearly not part of a future solution. Instead, corporate and business-unit executives should confront troubling questions about the attrition of marketing competence and find ways to restore it.[34]

Webster has identified the basic requirements for developing a market-driven, customer-focused business.[35] These requirements are as follows:

- Customer-oriented values and beliefs supported by top management.
- Integration of market and customer focus into the strategic-planning process.
- The development of strong marketing managers and programs.
- The creation of market-based measure of performance.
- The development of customer commitment throughout the organization.

Breman and Dalgic have identified the determinants or constructs of market orientation as below:[36]

- *Extroversion*: Continuously gathering market and environment information.
- *Holism*: Dissemination of this information within the organization. The whole organization should share this information.
- *Responsiveness*: Organization-wide responsiveness to this information.,
- *Long-term focus*: Long range, strategic focus within the context of optimization on long-term benefits, rather than on the maximization of short-term benefits.
- *Profit focus*: Profit motivation, aiming at profit-making objectives.
- *Relationship focus*: Establishing relationships and interaction with the customers.

To create superior customer value, Slater and Narver have suggested horizontal structures for the company, which are shown in Figure 4.3.

As shown in Figure 4.3, becoming a market-oriented company involves several interrelated requirements. According to the strategy author Craven there are four interrelated requirements.[38] They are as follows:

1. Information acquisition
2. Interfunctional assessment
3. Shared diagnosis and
4. Action.

Although several researchers with strategy and marketing background have used different terminologies, they reached similar conclusions in terms of the characteristics of a market orientation.

Market-oriented organizations are found to be learning organizations according to an empirical research.[39] According to Day,[40] becoming a learning organization helps an organization by providing an important capability for building competitive advantage. Learning organizations encourage open-minded inquiry, widespread information dissemination, and the use of mutually informed managers' visions about the current market and how it is likely to change in the future. In addition to these, a comprehensive management development program

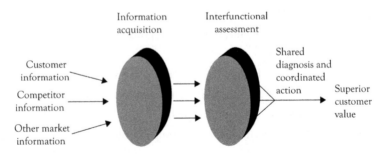

Figure 4.3. Market orientation.
Source: Adapted from Slater and Narver.[37]

has been proposed by Day.[41] The main steps to be taken in this program are as the follows:

- Diagnosis of current capabilities, using mapping and benchmarking methodologies.
- Anticipation of future needs for capabilities in light of the strategy for creating customer value.
- Bottom–up redesign, based on the formation of teams responsible for continuous improvement or radical redesign of underlying processes.
- Top–down direction from senior managers, who demonstrate a clear, continuing commitment to putting customers first.
- Use of information technology to enable the organization to do things it could not do before.
- Monitoring of progress toward improvement targets.[42]

The aim of market orientation is to provide superior customer value. As it can be seen from Figure 4.3, market orientation is based on obtaining information about customer, competitor, and the other market information. In addition to this, market orientation is related with deciding how to deliver superior customer value and taking actions to provide value to customers.

To sum up, becoming market oriented requires making major changes in the culture, processes, and structure of the traditional pyramid of organization. We can say that market-oriented organization has an important competitive advantage in providing customer value. In addition to these, market orientation helps to achieve superior performance for an organization.[43]

Ferrel and Hartline compared the traditional and market-oriented organizational structures by bring the frontline employees to the top of the company ladder, thus making the company very close to the customers.[44]

We can see the difference between traditional and market-oriented organization structure from Figure 4.4. As it can be understood from the figure traditional organization structure is more authoritative than market-oriented orientation structure.

In the Ferrel and Hartline market-oriented organization model, every level of the organization has its focus on serving customer needs and

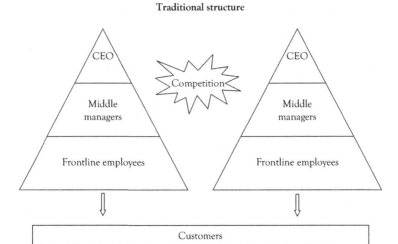

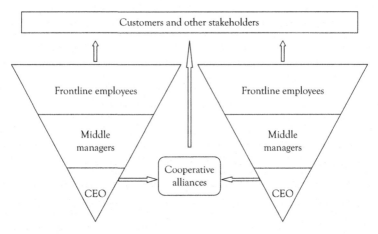

Figure 4.4. Traditional versus market-oriented organizational structures.
Source: Adapted from Ferrell and Hartline.[45]

wants. Each level serves the levels above it by taking any actions necessary to ensure that each level performs its job well. In this case, the role of the CEO is to ensure that his or her employees have everything they need to perform their jobs well. This mentality is valid at every level of the organization. Therefore, the job for a frontline manager is to ensure that frontline employees are capable and efficient. The aim of this effort is to meet customers' needs and wants.

Since the 1990s, several studies have been conducted by different people on the issue of becoming a market-oriented organization. In a way these authors have tried to "operationalize" the market orientation/ customer orientation strategy. Deshpande, Farley, and Webster; Jaworski and Kohli; Narver and Slater are a few to be mentioned in this regard.[46] Graves and Matsuno, in an unpublished but presented as an online research paper, have grouped these studies by giving the names as rational/mechanistic and organic perspectives. Table 4.1 shows their classifications.[47]

Marketing is the application of the firm's strategy in the marketplace which means market segmentation, customer targeting, and the positioning of the firm to its competitive strategy in a chosen area of business.[49] Earlier studies have indicated that the use of marketing as a strategy have had positive implications for a firm's performance as many researchers suggested.[50] Menon et al. also indicated that strategy planning as well as implementation was closely related with market orientation showing the strategic competence of the firm.

As Tokarczyk et al. (2007) observed, "the understanding of market orientation has increased, researchers have attempted to better discern the complex relationships among market orientation, firm performance, and a range of other constructs, such as innovation (Han, Kim, & Srivastava, 1998), entrepreneurship (Hurley & Hult 1998; Matsuno, Mentzer, & Rentz 2000), and the learning organization (Hurley & Hult 1998; Slater & Narver 1995)."[51]

Studies by Hurley and Hult (1998), Kohli and Jaworski (1990), Narver and Slater (1990), Slater and Narver (1998, 1999) indicated market orientation is largely the result of company culture as well as "sustainable competitive advantage."[52,53] As Tokarczyk et al. further observed, "A market-oriented company has dual vision in that it simultaneously maintains a focus on customers and the competition. Continuous monitoring of the competition allows firms to shift their operations to meet inroads from the competition. Internal discussions of competitor strengths and weaknesses allow the firm to counteract competitor strengths while simultaneously exploiting weaknesses."[54]

Further studies have supported the role of market orientation in the strategic management process. Hunt and Lambe (2000) and

Table 4.1. Rational/Mechanistic Perspective and Organic Perspective

	Objective/ mechanistic perspective	Subjective/ organic perspective	Organizational systems perspective
Authors	Barksdale and Darden (1971); Kohli and Jaworski (1990); Jaworski and Kohli (1993)	Webster (1988) Narver and Slater (1990); Deshpande, Farley, and Webster (1993); Slater and Narver (1994)	
Definition of market	Market orientation as implementation of activities	Market orientation as values and beliefs	Market orientation as values/beliefs and activities
Operationalization of market orientation	Intelligence-/ information-related activities	Organizational values and beliefs	Congruence between activities and values/ beliefs
Measures of market orientation	Behavioral measures	Cultural/ attitudinal measures	Composite measure
Relevance academic	Explicating structural relationships between market orientation, antecedents, and business performance	Investigating organization's cultural environment and its relation to business performance	More comprehensive view of the phenomenon. Highlights inconsistencies between behavioral and cognitive acceptance of MO
Managerial	Guideline of a set of specific behaviors	Management of cultural change	Balanced view of adoption processes
Disciplinary research tradition	Behavioral school of psychology, industrial organization economics	Anthropology, sociology	Organizational cognition
Research assumptions	Objective world -deterministic -rationality/ bounded rationality	Subjective world -idiosyncratic -metaphoric	Enacted world -Subjective attention-actions "create" "objective" reality
	Understand by decomposition	Understand shared meanings	Understand relationships between knowledge and action

Source: Graves and Matsuno.[48]

Hunt and Morgan (1995) conclude that market-oriented firms recognize the significance and value of utilizing customer and competitor knowledge in the development of business strategy.[55,56] Moreover, Tokarczyk et al. quoted from Kumar et al.[57,58] similar views. According to Dobni and Luffman "market orientation attunes organizations to the competitive environment, providing opportunities for strategic responses to environmental changes. The market orientation culture fosters behavioral characteristics that lead to behaviors that influence the establishment of the organization's strategic orientation."[59]

Authors Menon et al. defined marketing strategy making, a concept uniting the planning and implementation of marketing strategy, as a "complex set of activities, processes, and routines involved in the design and execution of marketing plans."[60] The firm's performance evaluation process established by these authors consisted of analyses of situation, comprehensiveness, emphasis of marketing assets and capabilities, cross-functional integration, communication quality, consensus commitment, and frontline staff interviews. Here situation analysis refers to the systematic analyses of a group's strengths, weakness, opportunity, and threats (SWOT) within the area of marketing strategy.[61] From this perspective, marketing strategy management is an application of the strategic management principles at the marketplace.

If we look at Figure 4.4, organization culture refers to a system of shared meaning held by members that distinguishes the organization from other organizations. Organizational culture is concerned with how employees perceive the characteristics of an organization's culture.[63] Cameron and Freeman have stated that "because cultures are defined by the values, assumptions, and interpretations of organization members, and because a common set of dimensions organizes these factors on both psychological and organizational levels, a model of culture types can be derived."[64] Some authors have classified cultures into four groups.[65] Other authors used the same classification.[66] The characteristics of the four culture types are as follows.

The clan culture is characterized by a very friendly working environment. Shared values and objectives, "we" consciousness, team thinking are typical for it. It has rather the character of an extended family than of a business entity. The managers play the role of the "parents" and loyalty or tradition pull the

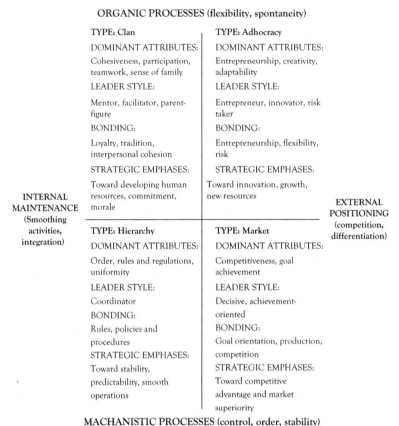

Figure 4.5. A model of organizational culture types.
Source: Adapted from Deshpande, Farley, and Webster (1993).[62]

company together. Long-time benefit of development of each individual is stressed here. A great importance is vested to solidarity, moral, working environment. The customers are considered the partners. Success is connected with the character of the internal climate and care for the employees. A clan culture, in which loyalty, tradition, and emphasis on internal maintenance could lead to a lack of attention to changing market needs.[67]

Hierarchical culture is connected with formalized and structured working environment, where procedures and regulations are pointed out. Formal rules represent the unifying element. In other words, the competing set of values is found in the hierarchical culture, which stresses order, rules, and regulations. The managers are good coordinators and organizers focused on effectiveness. Smooth running of the company is the most important factor. Stability and effectiveness are the supreme objectives.

Success is characterized as reliability of deliveries, smooth fulfillment of time schedules, low costs. Transactions are under the control of surveillance, evaluation, and direction. Business performance is defined by consistency and achievement of clearly stated goals.[68]

Adhocratic culture is characterized by dynamic business, creativity, and adaptability. Flexibility and tolerance are important beliefs and effectiveness is defined in terms of finding new markets and new directions for growth. In other words, experiments, innovative approach, thinking, and uniqueness put the company together. The managers are charged with support to individual initiative, freedom, and creativeness. Innovativeness and capability of adaptation to the turbulent environment is considered success.[69]

Market culture is characterized by competitiveness and goal achievement. In other words, the company that has market culture is a result-oriented company. Environment of the company is very competitive. Transactions are governed by market mechanism. The key measure of organizational effectiveness is productivity achieved through these market mechanisms. This culture type is in direct contrast to set of values expressed in a clan culture. The commitment of organizational members is ensured through participation, and organizational cohesiveness and personal satisfaction are rated more highly than financial and market share objectives. The managers request high performance, they are challenging and measurable and also objective oriented. Success is defined by acquisition of the market share and by market penetration.[70]

As noted by Webster, "A customer-oriented organizational culture is one in which the customer's interests come first, always. The firm stays focused on the customer in everything it does, and management constantly asks how it can do things better on behalf of the customer. The customer-oriented firm puts the customer's interests ahead of those of the owners, the management, and the employees. Everyone's job is defined in terms of how it helps to create and deliver value for the customer, and internal processes are designed and managed to ensure responsiveness to customer needs and maximum efficiency in value delivery. The customer-oriented firm is committed to relationship marketing, and employees work together to solve customer problems."[71]

According to Gebhardt, Carpenter, and Sherry, "the guiding coalitions perceived their existing firms' cultures as major impediments to organizational change and long-term success. Organization cultures before transformation were diverse, but they can be characterized as sharing the following attributes: a bureaucratic and internal focus; a reliance on historically successful approaches to solve new problems; highly structured routines parsed out by function and historical origin; employees identifying more with their function, job class, location, or other subgroup than with the overall organization; low levels of trust between groups within the organization; a lack of a common understanding of what the firm was trying to accomplish and how; passive aggressive behaviors due to the internal norms to be nice, coupled with the simultaneous use of covert methods to accomplish personal or group goals; and transactional leadership, defined by the extensive use of explicit rewards to manage employee behaviors."[72]

Kilman, Saxton, and Serpa (1985) and Schein (1992) provide the organizational culture definition for marketing as "the pattern of shared values and beliefs that help individuals understand organizational functioning and thus provide them norms for behavior in the organization."[73-75] This definition emphasizes three different parts of culture, including the following:

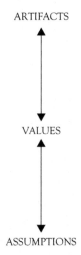

ARTIFACTS

VALUES

ASSUMPTIONS

Figure 4.6. Schein's (1984) model.
Source: Based on Hatch (1993).[77]

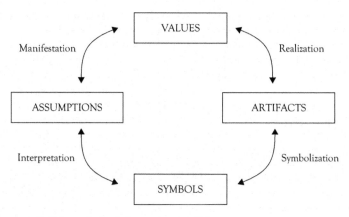

Figure 4.7. The cultural dynamics model.
Source: Adapted from Hatch.[81]

1. Values,
2. Norms, and
3. Behaviors in the organization.

Schein introduces an additional component of organizational culture, which he refers to as "artifacts."[76]

These artifacts include stories, arrangements, rituals, and language.[78] Schein emphasizes that artifacts are the most visible layer of organizational culture. Artifacts include stories, arrangements, rituals, and language that are created by an organization and have a strong symbolic meaning.[79]

Hatch proposes two fundamental changes to Schein's model (Figure 4.5). He comments "First, symbols are introduced as a new element. The introduction of symbols permits the model to accommodate the influences of both Schein's theory and symbolic-interpretive perspectives. Second, the elements of culture (assumptions, values, artifacts, and symbols) are made less central so that the relationships linking them become focal. This move initiates the shift from static to dynamic conceptions of culture, whereupon I reformulate Schein's theory in terms of dynamism by describing the relationships between cultural elements as processes" (Figure 4.6).[80]

Corporate culture   Market-oriented culture

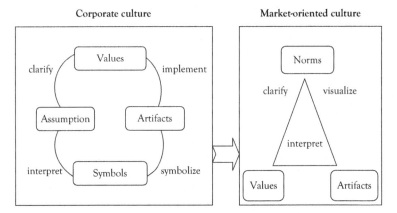

Figure 4.8. *Conceptualization of market-oriented culture based on Hatch's (1993) definition of corporate culture*
Source: Adapted from Yoon and Lee.[83]

Yoon and Lee have further developed Hatch's corporate culture and conceptualized the market orientation culture as Figure 4.7 explains:[82]

"The symbolic meaning of artifacts is more important than any instrumental function" (Hatch 1993) as Homburg and Pflesser in their comprehensive review on the subject concluded.[84]

The same researchers also pointed out the fact that organizational culture consists of four distinguishable but interrelated components as follows:

1. Shared basic values
2. Behavioral norms
3. Different types of artifacts
4. Behaviors.

Against this background, we conceptualize market-oriented organizational culture as a construct including the four components of the following:

1. Organization-wide shared basic values supporting market orientation,
2. Organization-wide norms for market orientation,
3. Perceptible artifacts of market orientation, and
4. The market-oriented behaviors.[85]

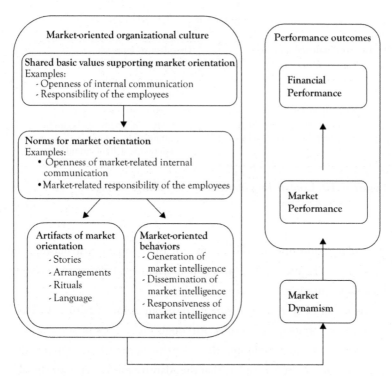

Figure 4.9. Market-oriented organizational culture
Source: Adapted from Homburg and Pflesser.[86]

Slater and Narver proposed two strategies to increase market orientation. One of the strategies is called the programmatic approach by Narver and Slater.[87] According to this approach, organizational change is the result of changes in the individual beliefs and behaviors. Thus, the focus is on the attitudes and activities of individuals.

The second approach is called the market-back approach. This is more of a continuous learning process where a business "continuously learns from its efforts to create buyer value and continuously adapts its structure, systems, staffing, etc., to reinforce its success and avoid repeating any failures." Under this approach, management and employees continuously learn from their efforts to create buyer value. They adjust strategy, structures, systems, and staffing based on such learning. According to Slater and Narver, the adaptive approach is superior to the programmatic approach for helping business become more market-oriented. The adaptive approach monitors results and

Top management leadership is absolutely essential.

The programmatic approach	The adaptive approach
• Top-down	• Bottom-up
• Big change	• Incremental change
• Structure-strategy-results	• Strategy-results-structure
• Program-oriented training	• Opportunity-oriented training
• Assumes culture change begins by changing individuals values	• Assume culture change begins by putting people into new roles that require new skills or attitudes

Figure 4.10. Contrasting approaches to culture change.
Source: Adapted from Slater and Narver.[89]

then makes appropriate adjustments in the company's structures and strategiesr.[88] Figure 4.10 depicts two alternative strategies to develop a market orientation.

As it can be seen from Figure 4.10, organization structure is shaped according to strategy and results. Although the programmatic approach is program-oriented training, the adaptive approach is opportunity-oriented training. So we can say that the adaptive program is more flexible and changeable to environmental conditions.

Chapter Summary

We believe that market orientation and its application in the market-place may show a difference between for an entirely new company and for an existing company to increase its market orientation. For the new company the requirements are easy to apply, but for an existing company it requires an implant which may take patience, time and change in the organization culture as well as training the personnel and several attempts to alter the ways the company did business.

The role of executives is also very important to become a market-oriented firm. Executives must encourage employees to understand consumer needs, wants, and demand. As it is mentioned earlier, consumer is the main point of business implementation in a market-oriented organization. Webster has suggested 15 guidelines for the market-driven manager.[90] They are as follows: (1) create customer focus throughout the business,

(2) listen to the customer, (3) define and nurture your distinctive competence, (4) define marketing as marketing intelligence, (5) target customers precisely, (6) manage for profitability, not sales volume, (7) make customer value the guiding star, (8) let the customer define quality, (9) measure and manage customer expectations, (10) build customer relationships and loyalty, (11) define the business as a service business, (12) commit to continuous improvement and innovation, (13) manage culture along with strategy and structure, (14) grow with partners and alliances, (15) destroy marketing bureaucracy.

CHAPTER 5

The Antecedents of Market Orientation

In Chapter 4, we discussed the market orientation for the new companies from the normative point of view by using previous research and lessons derived from the market examples. In this chapter, we will look at the antecedents of market orientation. The antecedents of market orientation are namely senior management characteristics, organizational characteristics, political behavior, and interdepartmental dynamics, which will be explained briefly.

A Company Case

J.D. Power® Recognizes USAA for Long-term Customer Satisfaction Results and Names USAA as a 2011 Customer Service Champion

USAA earned two significant customer service honors this week at the J.D. Power Customer Satisfaction Roundtable in Las Vegas.

10 Years of High Levels of Service

J.D. Power presented USAA with an exclusive recognition honoring "10 years of consistently high levels of customer satisfaction." According to J.D. Power President Finbarr O'Neill, the recognition is meant for organizations that consistently deliver on the promises they make to their customers.

"When we look across the many syndicated studies we conduct based on the voice of the customer, there are certain brands that stand out, year after year," commented O'Neill. "USAA has been one of the top performers in our studies for the past 10 years. This performance

(Continued)

(Continued)

makes it clear that this is a company that truly embraces the concept of continuous improvement in customer satisfaction."

"This honor means a lot to USAA because it recognizes our legendary commitment to serving our members," says Wayne Peacock, executive vice president of member experience at USAA. "It was earned by our 22,000 employees, who consistently act with passion to serve the military community and their families in an exceptional manner."

Source: https://www.usaa.com/inet/ent_blogs/Blogs?action=blogpost& blogkey=newsroom&postkey=two_prestigious_honors

In the market orientation literature, there are two key research subjects that are related to the study of market orientation. The first subject is the antecedents/barriers of market orientation.[1] The second subject is the consequences of market orientation.[2] Knowing the antecedents and consequences of market orientation is required to implement marketing strategies. For this reason, we will explain these two subjects in this book. In this chapter, the antecedents of market orientation will be explained while Chapter 8 will cover the consequences of market orientation.

The word antecedents refer to preceding circumstances. The antecedent factors impact market organization. These factors can encourage or discourage a market orientation. As stated by Kohli and Jaworski,[3] antecedents to a market orientation are the organizational factors that enhance or impede the implementation of the business philosophy represented by the marketing concept. In addition to these, we will focus on external factors that impact on achieving market orientation for a company. The antecedents of market orientation influence the market orientation either positively or negatively.

Senior Management Characteristics

Senior management characteristic is the most important factor for achieving market orientation. Several studies stress the critical role of senior managers in fostering a market orientation. Some author like Felton, Levitt, Webster, Kohli and Jaworski examined the role of senior management in achieving market orientation.[4] Senior management's encouragement is required to develop market orientation. In addition to management's mere involvement, the necessity of communicating a commitment to being market oriented has been dealt with extensively.[5]

Senior management's reinforcement of the importance of market orientation is likely to encourage employees to track changing markets, share market intelligence, and be responsive to market needs.[6] Therefore, "the greater the senior management emphasis on Market Orientation, the greater the market intelligence generation, the intelligence dissemination, and the responsiveness of the organization" they concluded. The introduction of new products and services is required for responding to changing market needs and wants. New products, services, and programs often run a high risk of failure and tend to be more recognizable and visible than established products. For this reason, "the greater the risk aversion of senior management, the lower the market intelligence generation, the intelligence dissemination, and the responsiveness of the organization."[7]

Felton stressed the importance of integration and coordination of all the marketing functions,[8] defining the marketing concept as "a corporate state of mind that insists on the integration and coordination of all the marketing functions, which, in turn, are melded with all other corporate functions, for the basic purpose of producing maximum long-range corporate profits." According to Felton, at this point, the role of senior management is very important. He stressed that "the board of directors, chief executives, and top-echelon executives appreciate the need to develop this marketing state of mind."[9] As Kohli and Jaworski concluded "the commitment of top managers is an essential prerequisite to a Market Orientation."[10] In addition to these, Levitt stressed that one of the factors that encourages the implementation of the marketing concept is the presence of "the right signals from the chief operating officer to the entire corporation regarding its continuing commitment to the marketing concept."[11] Levitt also suggests that continuous reinforcement by senior management is required if individuals within the organization are to be encouraged to generate, disseminate, and respond to market intelligence.

According to Craven, chief marketing executive's responsibilities related to business strategies include the following:[12]

- Participating in strategy formulation.
- Developing marketing strategies that follow business strategies.

Since these two responsibilities are closely interrelated, it is important to examine marketing's role and functions in both areas to gain more insight into marketing's responsibilities and contribution.

In his article titled *The Rediscovery of the Marketing Concept* article Webster explored the reasons for decline and resurgence of management interest in the marketing concept.[13] In addition to this, the role of CEO has been argued in implementing marketing. Webster stated that the customer-focused definition of the business must originate with top management, including the CEO and the heads of strategic operating units.[14]

According to the same author "customer oriented values and beliefs are uniquely the responsibility of top management. Only the chief executive officer (CEO) can take the responsibility for defining customer and market orientation as the driving forces, because if he doesn't customer first, he has, by definition, put something else, the interests of some other constituency or public first. Organization members will know what that is and behave accordingly."[15]

The internal barriers of market orientation application have been investigated by Tomaskova.[16] Tomaskova has stated that internal barriers of market orientation are closely connected to three elements. These elements are as follows:

1. Top management
2. Interfunctional coordination
3. Employees.

According to this author, only top management has special position from above elements, and has the main impact on market orientation. In addition to these, it has been stressed in this study that "the main barriers are connected with the top management and its skills such as the perception of market orientation, personality, knowledge, and experiences."[17]

As it can be observed in the previous explanation, the role of senior management is very important to gain market orientation. Senior management characteristics can be classified into four groups as follows:[18]

1. Top management emphasis
2. Risk aversion
3. Management training
4. Formal marketing education.

Top Management Emphasis

Dynamism in business environment caused by economic slowdown or growth, intense competition, globalization, mergers and acquisitions, rapid-fire product, and technological innovations challenges top managers' ability to sense and respond to market accurately. In other words, a manager's role is important to respond market changes. As stated by Kumar et al., it is critical that managers identify and understand strategic orientations that enable a firm to sustain performance, especially in the presence of rapid changes in market conditions.[19]

The role of top management in market-oriented organization has been examined by some researchers. Payne stated that if management's attitudes toward marketing are positive then a market orientation will emerge.[20] In a different study Jaworski and Kohli divided the antecedents of market orientation into three categories.[21] These antecedents are as follows:

1. Senior management factors
2. Interdepartmental dynamics
3. Organizational systems

These antecedents act as drivers or barriers of market orientation, resulting in some organizations being more market-oriented than others. Jaworski and Kohli showed that a "market orientation appears to be facilitated by the amount of emphasis top managers place on market orientation through continual reminders to employees that it is critical for them to be sensitive and responsive to market developments."[22]

Additionally, Slater and Narver also identified general guidelines for managers seeking to initiate customer value strategies.[23] And concluded that top management must play a facilitative role through the communication of certain guidelines and encourage contributions from employees.

Pulendran, Speed, and Widing(2000) in their market orientation study in Australia also identified a significant relationship between top management emphasis and overall market orientation.[24] They stated that "top management's actions can foster market-oriented activity through the provision of necessary training and resources, employee motivation and support, informal meetings with a focus on market-oriented activity and suggestion boxes to encourage the sharing of market based ideas."

Kirca, Jayachandran, and Beardenl have confirmed the results of importance of top management emphasis, interdepartmental connectedness, and market-based reward systems for the implementation of market orientation.[25]

Risk Aversion

The second component of senior management characteristics is risk aversion. Risk aversion has important implications. To offset the risks inherent in a commission-based wage, companies pay commissioned employees considerably more than they do those on straight salaries. Risk-averse employees will stick with the established way of doing their jobs, rather than taking a chance on innovative or creative methods.[26]

In the literature, the relationship between risk aversion of senior management and market orientation has been examined by several researchers.[27] According to Wood and Bhuian,[28] risk-averse managers tend to give information generation and dissemination low priority, have moderate track records with regard to market responsiveness.

Additionally, risk-averse managers do not encourage a market orientation. As stated by Jaworski and Kohli, changing market needs call for the introduction of innovative products and services to match the evolving needs. The introduction of new/modified offerings and programs is risky because the new offerings and programs may fail and may be resisted by risk averse managers.[29]

Kohli and Jaworski[30,31] assert that the symbolism viewed in senior management's willingness to take risks will encourage and facilitate organization-wide commitment to innovation and responsiveness. As they observed, "if top managers demonstrate a willingness to take risks and accept occasional failures as being natural, junior managers are more likely to propose and introduce new offerings in response to changes in customer needs. In contrast, if top managers are risk averse and intolerant of failures, subordinates are less likely to be responsive to changes in customer needs." In other words, a market orientation is related with a certain level of risk taking on the part of senior managers. In addition to these, senior managers should evaluate failure of new offerings as being a normal part of business life. According to Jaworski and Kohli, in the absence of such a willingness to take calculated risks, employees in the lower levels of an organizational hierarchy are unlikely to respond to market developments with new products, services, or programs.[32]

Bennet and O'Brien proposed that in learning-oriented organizations managers support staff development, encourage risk taking, and share insights and innovations.[33] Also, Han, Kim, and Srivastava examined this same subject and found that greater market orientation leads to higher degrees of risky and innovative behavior.[34] As Dalgic concluded, "a willingness of top management to take risks is, therefore, crucial for a market oriented company."[35]

Organizational Characteristics

The other antecedent set is organizational characteristics as Kohli and Jaworski labeled. A set of barriers to a market orientation briefly hinted at in the marketing literature is related to the structural form of organization.[36] Organizational characteristics include formalization, centralization, departmentalization, and reward systems. Kohli and Jaworski (1990), Jaworski and Kohli (1993) and Deshpande (1999) stated some hypotheses that are related with organization systems. These are as follows:[37]

- The greater the formalization of an organization, the less it will tend to generate, disseminate, and plan a response to market information but the more effective its response implementation.
- The greater the centralization of an organization, the less it will tend to generate, disseminate, and plan a response to market information but the more effective its response implementation.
- The greater the departmentalization of an organization, the less it will tend to generate, disseminate, and plan a response to market information but the more effective its response implementation.
- The greater the reliance on market-based factors in evaluating and rewarding managers, the greater the generation, the dissemination, and the response of the organization to market intelligence.

Formalization and centralization have been examined by some researchers in the marketing literature.[38] Formalization is the degree to which the final decision results from a series of logically planned activities that are tightly controlled.[39]

According to Hall, Haas, and Johnson,[40] formalization is the degree to which rules define roles, authority relations, communications, norms and sanctions, and procedures. In other words, formalization refers to the degree to which jobs within the organization are standardized. If a job is a highly formalized, the incumbent has a minimum amount of discretion over what, when, and how to do it. Employees can be expected to always handle the same input in exactly the same way, resulting in a consistent and uniform output. As it can be understood from above explanations, if a firm has a high formalization, there are explicit job descriptions, lots of organizational rules, and clearly defined procedures covering work processes. However, if a firm has a low formalization, job behaviors are relatively unprogrammed, and employees have a great deal of freedom to exercise discretion in their work.[41]

According to Aiken and Hage, centralization is the delegation of decision-making authority throughout an organization and the extent of participation by organizational members in decision-making.[42] Centralization has been redefined by Robbins and Judge as follows: "Centralization refers to the degree to which decision-making is concentrated at a single point in the organization. In centralized organizations, top managers make all the decisions, and lower level managers merely carry out their directives."[43] The authors state that the concept of centralization includes only formal authority, that is, the rights inherent in a position.

Jaworski and Kohli founded that there is negative relationship between centralization and market orientation.[44] This result suggests that it may be useful to "empower" employees to make decisions at lower levels of organizations rather than concentrate decision-making in the upper level of an organization. The negative relationship between both centralization and formalization and overall market orientation was substantiated by Harris.[45]

"Departmentalization refers to the number of departments into which organizational activities are segregated and compartmentalized" as defined by Jaworski and Kohli.[46] According to Robbins and Judge, the basis by which jobs are grouped is called departmentalization.[47] Once jobs are divided by work specialization, they must be grouped so common tasks can be grouped. In sum, departmentalization may depend on the business what to do. In addition to these, the type of product or services, the geography, the particular type of customer can be used to departmentalize the jobs.

Reward System

Literature on the subject of rewarding suggests that measurement/reward systems are instrumental in shaping the behaviors of employees.[48] As Webster stated, "the key to developing a market-driven, customer orientated business lies in how managers are evaluated."[49] According to Jaworski and

Kohli, if managers are primarily evaluated on the basis of short-term profitability and sales, they are likely to focus on these criteria and neglect market factors such as customer satisfaction that assure the long-term health of an organization.[50]

It also seems likely that if managers are evaluated and rewarded by market-related factors, this will have a positive influence on a market orientation. This means that the greater the reliance on market-based factors for evaluating and rewarding managers, the greater the market intelligence generation, the intelligence dissemination, and the responsiveness of the organization.[51]

Sigauw, Brown, and Widing in their research concluded that market-based reward systems were essential in achieving market orientation.[52] Furthermore, the research on this subject showed that the type of reward system significantly reduces role conflict and job ambiguity.

The evaluation of employee performance through sales volume, short-term profitability, and rate of return measures led them to focus solely on these aspects of performance to the exclusion of market factors such as customer satisfaction and service levels. By comparison, organizations that evaluate and administer rewards based on customer satisfaction and service levels are more likely to encourage the active generation and dissemination of market intelligence and responsiveness to market needs.[53]

Political Behavior

Political behavior consists of individuals' attempts to promote self-interests and threaten others' interests.[54] Kohli and Jaworski have suggested that "political structure norm is an informal system that reflects the extent to which members of an organization view political behavior in the organization as being acceptable. A market orientation calls for a concerted response by the various departments of an organization to market intelligence. A highly politicized system, however, has the potential for engendering interdepartmental conflict."[55] Harris and Piercy found a negative relationship between market orientation and political behavior of retailing companies.[56] For this reason, an organization which becomes market-oriented firm should try to decrease political behavior.

Interdepartmental Dynamics

The other antecedent of market orientation is interdepartmental dynamics. Interdepartmental dynamics have been defined by Kohli and Jaworski as, "the formal and informal interactions and relationship among organization's departments."[57] They classified interdepartmental dynamics into two groups namely:

1. Interdepartmental conflict
2. Interdepartmental connectedness.

Interdepartmental Conflict

Interdepartmental conflict has been examined by some researchers in the literature.[58] Levitt emphasized that interdepartmental conflict may be mischievous (harmful) to the implementation of market orientation.[59] Interdepartmental conflict also has impact on communication, secrecy, and in-bred competition. As stated by Dutton and Walton interdepartmental conflict may result in reduced interfunctional performance.[60]

A certain amount of interdepartmental conflict will affect the sharing and the responsiveness of relevant market information.[61] As Desphande observes, "an important factor is interdepartmental conflict, for example tension and conflict among departments arising from the incompatibility of actual or desired responses."[62] It can be concluded that the greater the interdepartmental conflict, the lower the market intelligence dissemination and the responsiveness of the organization.

While some level of interdepartmental conflict is inherent in the charters of the different departments, it appears useful to reduce the level of conflict by using the various means such as interdepartmental training programs, cross-functional activities, and alignment of departmental performance objectives by focusing them on markets (e.g., customer satisfaction.[63] They also concluded that "interdepartmental conflict, or the tension between departments that arises from divergent goals, inhibits concerted responses to market needs and thus diminishes market orientation."

Interdepartmental Connectedness

The other component of interdepartmental dynamics is interdepartmental connectedness. This variable refers to the degree of direct formal or informal contact among employees across departments.[64] Market orientation by leading to greater sharing and use of information.[65] As stated by Deshpande, the greater the interdepartmental connectedness, the greater the market intelligence dissemination and the responsiveness of the organization.[66] Interdepartmental connectedness has also been studied by several authors.[67] These researches suggest that interdepartmental connectedness encourages interaction and utilization of the information. Thus, it can be expected that the greater the extent to which individuals across departments are directly connected, the more they are likely to exchange market intelligence and respond to it in a concerted fashion.[68] Interdepartmental connectedness examined by Deshpande and Zaltman also concluded that interdepartmental connectedness is positively related with intelligence dissemination and responsiveness.[69]

According to Kohli and Jaworski, interdepartmental dynamics (connectedness and conflict) have a key role in influencing the dissemination of and responsiveness to market intelligence.[70] These authors have recommended some inexpensive ways to manage these two dynamics (connectedness and conflict). These ways are interdepartmental lunches, sports leagues that require mixed department teams, and newsletters that "poke fun" at various interdepartmental relations. In addition, Kohli and Jaworski have recommended more advanced efforts. These are exchange of employees across departments, cross-department training programs, and senior department managers spending a day with executives in other departments. Such efforts and activities appear to foster an understanding of the personalities of managers in other departments, their culture, and their particular perspectives.[71]

Chapter Summary

In the market-orientation literature, there are two key research subjects that are related to the study of market orientation. The first subject is the antecedents/barriers of market orientation. The second subject is the consequences of market orientation. Knowing the antecedents and consequences of market orientation is required to implement marketing strategies. For this reason, we will explain these both subjects.

The word antecedents refer to preceding circumstances. The antecedent factors impact market organization. These factors can encourage or discourage a market orientation. As stated by Kohli and Jaworski, antecedents to a market orientation are the organizational factors that enhance or impede the implementation of the business philosophy represented by the marketing concept. The antecedents of market orientation influence the market orientation either positively or negatively.[72]

Senior management characteristic is the most important factor for achieving market orientation. Dynamism in business environment caused by economic slowdown or growth, intense competition, globalization, mergers and acquisitions, rapid-fire product, and technological innovations challenges top managers' ability to sense and respond to market accurately. In other words, a manager's role is important to respond market changes. The second component of senior management characteristics is risk aversion. Risk aversion has important implications.

The other antecedent set is organizational characteristics. Organizational characteristics include formalization, centralization, departmentalization, and reward systems. The other antecedent of market orientation is interdepartmental dynamics. Interdepartmental dynamics can be classified into two groups, namely, interdepartmental conflict and interdepartmental connectedness.

CHAPTER 6

Implanting Market Orientation in Organizations

In this chapter, we will tackle the issue of implementing market orientation for the existing companies. In other words, we will explain how to implant market orientation in organizations. In this context, a guideline for implanting market orientation, action plan for implementation, and four-stage formulas to create a market orientation will be explained.

A Company Case

American Express Ranks Highest in Credit Card Customer Satisfaction for a Fourth Consecutive Year

WESTLAKE VILLAGE, Calif.: 19 August 2010—Overall customer satisfaction with credit cards has rebounded from a three-year low in 2009, but professed loyalty continues to slip as skepticism that card issuers are focused on customers' best interests remains, according to the J.D. Power and Associates 2010 U.S. Credit Card Satisfaction Study[SM] released today.

Overall credit card satisfaction in 2010 averages 714 on a 1,000-point scale, up 9 points from 705 in 2009. However, customers who say they "definitely will not switch" primary cards in the next 12 months continues to decline, averaging 22 percent in 2010, down from 25 percent in 2009 and 30 percent in 2008. While customers perceive card issuers as "financially stable" and even "reliable," they are significantly less likely to view them as "customer driven."

American Express ranks highest in customer satisfaction for a fourth consecutive year with a score of 769 and performs well across all six factors that drive satisfaction. Discover Card follows with a score of 757 and performs particularly well in the interaction factor. U.S.

(*Continued*)

(Continued)

Bank ranks third with a score of 727. The common denominators of performance among the highest-ranked issuers are exceptional rewards and benefits offerings; superior service experiences across phone and online channels; and a focus on reducing problems and resolving those that do occur with minimum time and effort for customers.

The 2010 U.S. Credit Card Satisfaction Study is based on responses from more than 8,500 credit card customers. The study was fielded in May and June 2010.

Source: http://businesscenter.jdpower.com/news/pressrelease.aspx? ID=2010159

As stated by Dalgic, while the theoretical arguments in favor of following a market orientation are clear in practice, it seems extremely difficult to implant such an approach in an organization. He has suggested some important requirements to implant market orientation in organization. These are as follows:[1]

- *A strategic vision and long-term commitment:* Market orientation is a continuous, strategic commitment. The decision to implant a market orientation into an existing or a start-up business requires the support of the entire organization. According to him, these strategies may require conscientious efforts, carefully detailed analysis, well-planned, realistically timetables, and sensitively applied and controlled methods. It may be concluded that a solid reputation in the minds of the customers is essential to be successful as a marketer.[2]
- *Managing the change for market orientation:* Implanting a market orientation strategy may require several changes within an organization. Analyzing the current system and behavior, and preparing a detailed plan for the norm structure that will support the degree of marketing orientation require changes in the planning and execution of firm's strategic marketing activities. These changes should be planned and implemented. Management should develop methods to influence the behavior of the people by rewarding the good

ones. Top management commitment and exemplary behavior support the emergence of new norms because they reinforce the transmission of norms between individuals, stories, rituals, and symbols. In this process internal marketing may be useful to implant a market orientation in a company.

A Guideline for Implanting Market Orientation

A guideline for implanting market orientation has been suggested by Dalgic that are follows:[3]

- "Put the CEO and the top management team in charge of the process.
- Ensure that the reason for change toward market orientation is clearly communicated to every individual in the firm by every means of communication.
- Create an internal environment for consultation and feedback.
- Take time to finish the total change process including the feedback stage.
- Involve employees and give them freedom to work out the change for their own functional areas.
- Provide training in new values, work methods, and customer understanding and service quality improvement.
- Acknowledge and reward the successful employees."

Action Plan for Implementation

The following is a guideline toward achieving the changes in the organizational culture that requires implanting market orientation.[4]

- "Establishing a market intelligence system and its related departments equipped with human, physical, and financial resources, directed to the market environment to collect information.
- Developing and implementing a method of information dissemination that will be responsible for the distribution and interpretation of the market intelligence.

- Creating an informal, flexible, active communication system between and among departments in a supportive manner, reducing the bureaucracy within the company, supporting bottom–up information flows as well as top–down ones.
- Establishing market-based reward and payment systems, as well as internal communication system.
- Abolishing formal structures and establishing market-based departments and project teams.
- Planning for an internal marketing system to present the market orientation strategy to the company personnel.
- Planning company-based training programs aimed at creating customer sensitivity, service quality-improvement programs, and customer understanding strategies.
- Establishing a customer retention philosophy within the company.
- Preparing for a relationship marketing strategy, depending upon the size of the company.
- Adopting one-to-one marketing with big customers, and building niches around customers.
- Applying total quality management and periodical service quality surveys among management and customers.
- Setting up customer helplines.
- Undertaking customer satisfaction surveys about both goods and services and action upon the results."

Based on the research of three US academics, Gebhardt, Carpenter, and Sherry, "Walking The Walk" approach was suggested as a new way of changing company culture to apply market orientation.[5] Their research findings were posted at the Kellogg Business School at the following link: http://insight.kellogg.northwestern.edu/index.php/Kellogg/article/walking_the_walk.

By referring to the Intel CEO's announcement of "every idea and technical solution should be focused on meeting customers' needs from the outset," they commented that "he was proposing a radical shift from an organization focused on microprocessor design to a company whose culture would prioritize understanding and meeting specific customer needs. As more firms make the effort to become customer focused, it is important to comprehend not only what a market orientation is, but also how such a transformation occurs."[6]

In their research Gebhardt, Carpenter, and Sherry tried to find an answer to the question "How does a firm implement the cultural changes that will make customers a top priority in its organization?"[7] To answer this question they suggested "to get an up-close look at companies in different stages of organizational change." They proposed a four-stage formula for creating a market orientation.

Their formula requires employing several qualitative research methods such as "oral histories, ethnographies, and historical documents." They used several qualitative research methods to "examine seven firms that were just beginning to adopt a greater market orientation, already in the process of such a change, or had recently completed the transformation. Over a period of 10 months, theses researchers conducted formal interviews with 70 employees; spent more than 40 days observing and speaking with employees in executive meetings, during meals, and in company work and break areas; and reviewed hundreds of historical documents such as annual reports, press releases, and industry publications."[8]

Figure 6.1 illustrates their four-stage formula in the process of creating a market orientation:

1. Initiation
2. Reconstitution
3. Institutionalization
4. Maintenance.

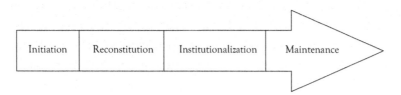

Figure 6.1. Four-stage formula to create a market orientation.
Source: Adapted from Gebhardt, Carpenter, and Sherry (2009).[9]

Their research conclusion can be outlined as follows:

1. During initiation, executives or other powerful stakeholders first recognize an external threat to the company (such as failure to meet financial performance targets) and then prepare to implement a market orientation by identifying specific initiatives for the transformation process.

2. The reconstitution involves presenting the plan to the entire organization simultaneously. The plan should describe the values that have been selected to guide the firm's behavior, as well as the specific change initiatives that will occur. After presenting the plan, the firm can promote an organization-wide understanding of how cultural values affect the company's ability to meet market needs by sending cross-functional teams to meet with customers and other key stakeholders. Ultimately, personnel who are unwilling to support the cultural transformation are replaced by new hires who share the values important to the organization.

3. The third stage, institutionalization, occurs as a market-oriented culture becomes formally incorporated throughout the organization. Employee rewards are aligned with the firm's performance in the marketplace; training is designed to reinforce cultural values; and decision-making power is decentralized and extended to all members of the organization.

4. Finally, during the maintenance stage, the company protects its market-oriented culture from deterioration by screening new hires to ensure they fit the restructured image; creating activities that remind employees of the process of cultural change the company has undergone; and staying connected to the market through research and field visits.

They concluded that "although firms may 'talk the talk' of a market orientation, companies can 'walk the walk' by successfully implementing cultural change designed to focus organizational efforts on meeting customer needs."

Narver, Slater, and Tietje in a different research entitled "Creating a Market Orientation" using Kotter's eight essential leadership steps for effecting organizational transformation developed an eight-step leadership guideline adapted to the context of creating a market orientation:[10,11]

1. Establish a sense of urgency in the organization for creating a market orientation.

2. Form a powerful guiding coalition for creating a market orientation.

3. Create a vision of a market orientation and a plan for its implementation.

4. Communicate the vision of a market orientation.

5. Empower others to act on the vision.

6. Plan for and create short-term market wins.

7. Consolidate improvements based on the market performance and produce even more change.

8. Institutionalize continuous learning and improvement in attracting, retaining, and growing targeted customers.

According to Payne, "successful development of a marketing orientation requires a thorough understanding of the culture of the organization and a carefully constructed program of management development, support activities, and follow-up overcome the organizational inertia that can impede the transition to marketing effectiveness."[12] Payne also suggested a program that can increase market orientation.

1. Understanding the mix of potentially conflicting orientations in the organization.

2. Identifying the present levels of marketing effectiveness.

3. Implementing a plan to improve market orientation.

The implementation of market orientation seems to be difficult. Top management commitment is the first prerequisite for the implementation of market orientation. Other important aspects are the involvement of all functional departments, human resource department, and adequate marketplace information.[13]

Lear's centralized approach (common in multidivisional companies) for achieving economy and efficiency could be instrumental for achieving market orientation. Lear has suggested three steps that are shown below:[14]

1. *Centralized headquarters*: Having all division management staff in one city and building makes it easier for the managers to meet and discuss coordinated marketing plans.

2. *Consolidated field sales offices*: When district managers of different divisions are remote from one another, even though they may be in the same city, it is unrewarding to attempt coordinated marketing

programming. When they are lodged together, it becomes more feasible for them to conduct joint campaigns, share specialized market personnel, and plan out local strategy for selling whole markets as opposed to directing sales efforts along straight sales territorial lines.

3. *Centralized marketing staffs*: By drawing together into one centralized division many of the primary staff marketing functions (advertising, market research, physical distribution, and so on), it is possible to introduce a coordinated marketing concept in the planning phase of marketing work.

According to Lear, "the key role in developing market-oriented plans and in seeing that the plans are effectively carried out, must be played by the chief marketing executive."[15]

Some authors have attempted to identify the reasons that hinder (barrier) market orientation in some companies. The barriers have been stated by Masiello are as follows:[16]

1. Most functional areas in the company do not understand the concept of being truly driven by the market needs.
2. Most employees do not know how to translate their classical functional responsibilities into market-responsive actions.
3. Most functional areas do not understand the roles of the other functions in the company.
4. The employees in each functional area do not have meaningful input to the marketing directions of the company although they are often closest to the operational characteristics of the marketplace.

Webster has also illustrated the barriers in becoming market oriented:[17]

1. An incomplete understanding of the marketing concept itself.
2. The inherent conflict between short-term and long-term sales and profit goals.
3. An overemphasis on short term, financially oriented measures of management performance.
4. Top management's own values and priorities concerning the relative importance of customers and the firm's other constituencies.

Webster also commented "the marketing strategy is an extension and implementation of corporate and business strategies, and it focuses on the definition and the selection of markets and customers to be served and the continual improvement, in performance and cost, of products to be offered in those markets. In a market driven, customer-oriented business, the key elements of the business plan will be a focus on well-defined market segments and the firm's unique competitive advantage in those segments."[18]

As it can be understood from the above explanations, achieving market orientation cannot be possible for some companies. Despite the evidence that a market orientation boosts performance, many companies around the world are not focused on their customers or competitors. The reasons will be explained below.[19]

1. Competitive conditions may enable a company to be successful in the short run without being particularly sensitive to customer desires.
2. Different levels of economic development across industries or countries may favor different business philosophies.
3. Companies can suffer from strategic inertia—the automatic continuation of strategies successful in the past, even though current market conditions are changing.

As mentioned earlier, the degree of adoption of a market orientation varies not only across companies but also across entire industries. Industries that are in the earlier stages of their life cycles, or that benefit from barriers to entry or other factors reducing the intensity of competition, are likely to have relatively fewer market-oriented firms.

Mullins and Walker commented that "in some cases, a firm that achieved success by being in tune with its environment loses touch with its market because managers become reluctant to tamper with strategies and marketing programs that worked in the past. Managers begin to believe there is one best way to satisfy their customers. Such strategic inertia is dangerous because customers need to competitive offering change over time."[20]

One author, Dalgic, classified the market-oriented companies using a medical analogy. He observed and developed a model that there were two distinct organization types on the basis of market orientation. regarding their market orientation: one group can be labeled as Type A, the other as Type B.[21]

A-type firms exhibit a purer form of market orientation, and embody a genuine philosophy that generating satisfied customers and satisfactory profits are not mutually incompatible goals and that, in fact, they are the only long-term goals that make business sense. They are "learning organization," as Slater and Narver put it.[22] "A-type firms are likely to be small and growing, to have strong leadership and culture, to be innovative, lean, and flexible. A-type firms focus on relationships, and the lifetime value of the customer," Dalgic comments.

B-type firms, on the other hand, see market orientation as a "magic bullet solution" to external pressures, particularly increased competition, a more expensive modus operandi to be used only when necessary and in order to stay one step ahead of the competition. This group of firms regards market orientation as a corporate stage of evolution, brought about by external pressures, particularly competition. The B-type firm is driven by cost considerations and by competitor analysis. It is likely to be large, bureaucratic, and reactive, according to Dalgic in his book published in the *Oxford Book of Marketing*.[23]

While B-type firms are obsessed with benchmarking their offerings against competitors, A-type firms attempt to satisfy their customers to the point where a loyalty exists and the company effectively eliminates competitors by domesticating the relevant market, so that the price-driven microeconomic paradigm no longer applies.[24] Dalgic further comments:[25] "This (A-type/B-type) distinction may account for the two schools of thought regarding the definitions of market orientations: one (Day and Wensley 1988; Narver and Slater 1990) includes "focus on competitors" explicitly; the other (Kohli and Jaworski 1990; Jaworski and Kohli 1993) does not include separate reference to the competitor in the list of attributes or exhibited processes in the market-oriented firms, but rather includes competitor intelligence in a broader category of market intelligence including competitors, customers, and stakeholders. These two organizations types of market orientation are compared." Figure 6.2 compares these two types of market-oriented companies.

A type	B type
Genuine market orientation philosophy	Customer orientation accepted when market forces require it
Belief that profits come from satisfied customers	Emphasis on cost cutting and profit maximization
Learning organization	Learning only when competitors make it necessary
Customer/competitors/ stakeholders/technology-based market information generation	Competitor-based market information generation
Lean, mean, flexible	Large, bureaucratic
Strong relationship and organization culture for customer care	Change in organization culture
Innovative	Imitative
Long-term focus	Short-term focus

Figure 6.2. Two types of organization for market orientation model developed by Dalgic.

Chapter Summary

While the theoretical arguments in favor of following a market orientation are clear in practice, it seems extremely difficult to implant such an approach in an organization.[26] He has suggested some important requirements to implant market orientation in organizations. These requirements are a strategic vision and long-term commitment and managing the change for market orientation. Market orientation is a continuous, strategic commitment. The decision to implant a market orientation into an existing or a start-up business requires the support of the entire organization. To implant a market orientation strategy may require several changes within an organization. Analyzing the current system and behavior and preparing a detailed plan for the norm structure that will support the degree of marketing orientation require changes in the planning and execution of firm's strategic marketing activities. These changes should be planned and implemented. Management should develop methods to influence the behavior of the people by rewarding the good ones. Top management commitment and exemplary behavior support the emergence of new norms because they reinforce the transmission of norms between individuals, stories, rituals, and symbols. In this process, internal marketing may be useful to implant a market orientation in a company.

Gebhardt, Carpenter, and Sherry suggested a four-stage formula in the process of creating a market orientation. These are initiation, reconstitution, institutionalization, and maintenance.[27]

One author, Dalgic, classified the market-oriented companies using a medical analogy. Dalgic observed and developed a model that there were two distinct organization types regarding their market orientation: one group can be labeled as Type A and the other as Type B.[28]

A-type firms exhibit a purer form of market orientation, and embody a genuine philosophy that generating satisfied customers and satisfactory profits are not mutually incompatible goals and that, in fact, they are the only long-term goals that make business sense. B-type firms on the other hand see market orientation as a "magic bullet solution" to external pressures, particularly increased competition, a more expensive modus operandi to be used only when necessary and in order to stay one step ahead of the competition. This group of firms regards market orientation as a corporate stage of evolution, brought about by external pressures, particularly competition.

CHAPTER 7

Measurement of Market Orientation

In Chapter 6, we explained how to implant market orientation in organizations. In this context, a guideline for implanting market orientation, action plan for implementation, and four-stage formula to create a market orientation were explained. In this chapter, we will look at an extensive set of scales. In this context, three major scales will be explained. These three scales are reliable and valid. Additionally, these scales have been applied commonly in the marketing literature.

A Company Case

QVC Continues to Be Recognized for Exceptional Customer Service

West Chester, PA. (January 12, 2011)—QVC announced today that it has once again secured a top 10 spot in the annual NRF Foundation/ American Express® Customers' Choice survey. The survey asked more than 9,000 shoppers to identify the leading retailers who provide the very best customer service.

"The QVC team is thrilled to be recognized by consumers as one of the 10 best customer service retailers in the country for the third year in a row," said Dan McDermott, QVC's senior vice president of customer services. "We are committed to providing our customers with exceptional customer service each and every day."

"Consumers have spoken and QVC's customer service has received a ringing endorsement," said Katherine Mance, executive director, NRF Foundation. "So many things are important when it comes to providing great customer service, such as helpful and knowledgeable

(Continued)

(Continued)

staff and accommodating return policies. This award recognizes all of QVC's hard work in these and other areas."

The NRF ranking is one of a number of customer service honors QVC received in recent weeks. In fact, the multimedia retailer has been recognized by both Gomez, the web performance division of Compuware, and the ForeSee E-retail Satisfaction Index for its excellence in customer service during the holiday shopping season.

About QVC

QVC, Inc., a wholly owned subsidiary of Liberty Media Corporation attributed to the Liberty Interactive Group (Nasdaq: LINTA), is one of the largest multimedia retailers in the world. QVC is committed to providing its customers with thousands of the most innovative and contemporary beauty, fashion, jewelry, and home products. Its programming is distributed to approximately 195 million homes worldwide. The company's website, QVC.com, is ranked among the top general merchant Internet sites. With operations in the United Kingdom, Germany, Japan and Italy, West Chester, PA.-based QVC has shipped more than a billion packages in its 24-year history.

Source: http://www.qvc.com/PressRelease.content.html?press=cp
_press_011211_cust_serv.endpress

Different market orientation scales have been developed by different researchers. The measurement of market orientation is important because company can learn its position in terms of market orientation by this way and make necessary changes in its strategies. If we consider the empirical research results in the literature, being market oriented or not may play a vital role in the company strategy as well as organization structure and organization culture.

In the marketing literature, there are three important scales that are used for measuring market orientation. These scales are commonly tested in marketing literature and are considered to be valid and reliable. These scales can be a guide for practical applications for companies. These scales are as follows:

1. The first scale is MARKOR (a measure of market orientation), a scale developed by Kohli, Jaworski, and Kumar in 1993.[1]
2. The second scale MKTOR was developed by Narver and Slater in 1990.[2]
3. The third scale was developed by Deshpande, Farley, and Webster in 1993.[3]

These scales will be explained briefly as follows:

MARKOR (a measure of market orientation) is one of very early scales developed and used to measure market orientation. This scale is a refined version of Jaworski and Kohli's scale,[4] and was published in 1993 by Kohli, Jaworski, and Kumar, and named as MARKOR. Key features of this scale are the following:[5]

1. An expanded focus on market rather than customer intelligence.
2. An emphasis on a specific form of interfunctional coordination with respect to market intelligence.
3. A focus on activities related to intelligence processing rather than the effect of these activities (e.g., profitability).

The second scale was developed by Narver and Slater which is a 15-item factor-weighted scale.[6] In this study, Narver and Slater hypothesized that market orientation is a one-dimensional construct consisting of three behavioral components and two decision criteria:

1. Customer orientation
2. Competitor orientation
3. Interfunctional coordination
4. Long-term focus, and a
5. Profit objective.

Each of the above items can be measured with reliability using a multi-item scale. The authors stressed that for a business to maximize its

Table 7.1. Market Orientation Scale (MARKOR)

Scale Items	Strongly disagree	Disagree	Neither agree nor disagree	Agree	Strongly agree
Intelligence Generation					
In this business unit, we meet customers at least once a year to find out what products or services they will need in the future.	1	2	3	4	5
Individuals from our manufacturing department interact directly with customers to learn how to serve them better.	1	2	3	4	5
In this business unit, we do a lot of in-house market research.	1	2	3	4	5
We are slow to detect changes in our customers' product preferences (R).	1	2	3	4	5
We poll end users at least once a year to assess the quality of our products and services.	1	2	3	4	5
We often talk with or survey those who can influence our end users' purchases (e.g., retailer, distributors)*.	1	2	3	4	5
We collect industry information by informal means (e.g., lunch with industry friends, talk with trade partners).	1	2	3	4	5
In this business unit, intelligence on our competitors is generated independently by several departments.	1	2	3	4	5
We are slow to detect fundamental shifts in our industry (e.g., competition, technology, and regulation) (R)*.	1	2	3	4	5
We periodically review the likely effect of changes in our business environment (e.g., regulation) on consumers*.	1	2	3	4	5

Intelligence Dissemination

A lot of informal "hall talk" in this business unit concerns our competitors' tactics or strategies*.	1	2	3	4	5
We have interdepartmental meetings at least once a quarter to discuss market trends and developments*.	1	2	3	4	5
Marketing personal in our business unit spend time discussing customers' future needs with other functional departments.	1	2	3	4	5
Our business unit periodically circulates documents (e.g., reports, newsletters) that provide information on our customers*.	1	2	3	4	5
When something important happens to a major customer of market, the whole business unit knows about it within a short period*.	1	2	3	4	5
Data on customer satisfaction are disseminated at all levels in this business unit on a regular basis.	1	2	3	4	5
There is minimal communication between marketing and manufacturing departments concerning market developments (R).	1	2	3	4	5
When one department finds out something important about competitors, it is slow to alert other departments (R)*.	1	2	3	4	5

Responsiveness

It takes us forever to decide how to respond to our competitor's price changes (R).	1	2	3	4	5
Principles of market segmentation drive new product development efforts in this business unit.	1	2	3	4	5

(Continued)

Table 7.1. Market Orientation Scale (MARKOR) (Continued)

	1	2	3	4	5
For one reason or another we tend to ignore changes in our customer's product or service needs (R).	1	2	3	4	5
Our business plans are driven more by technological advances than by market research (R).	1	2	3	4	5
Several departments get together periodically to plan a response to changes taking place in our business environment.	1	2	3	4	5
The product lines we sell depends more on internal politics than real market needs (R)*.	1	2	3	4	5
If a major competitor were to launch an intensive campaign targeted at our customers, we would implement a response immediately.	1	2	3	4	5
The activities of the different departments in this business unit are well coordinated*.	1	2	3	4	5
Customer complaints fall on deaf ears in this business unit (R)*.	1	2	3	4	5
Even if we come up with a great marketing plan, we probably would not be able to implement in a timely fashion (R)*.	1	2	3	4	5
We are quick to respond to significant changes in our competitors' pricing structures*.	1	2	3	4	5
When we find out that customers are unhappy with the quality of our service, we take corrective action immediately*.	1	2	3	4	5
When we find that customers would like us to modify a product of service, the departments involved make concerted efforts to do so*.	1	2	3	4	5

(R) denotes reverse coded item.
* Refers to addition of item during or after completion of the second pretest.

Table 7.2. Narver and Slater Scale of Market Orientation

	Not at all	To a very slight extent	To a small extent	To a moderate extent	To a considerable extent	To a great extent	To an extreme extent
	1	2	3	4	5	6	7
1. Our salespeople regularly share information within our business concerning competitor's strategies.							
2. Our business objectives are driven primarily by customer satisfaction.							
3. We rapidly respond to competitive actions that threaten us.							
4. We constantly monitor our level of commitment on orientation to serving customer needs.							
5. Our top managers from every function regularly visit our current and prospective customers.							
6. We freely communicate information about our successful and unsuccessful customer experiences across all business functions.							
7. Our strategy for competitive advantage is based on our understanding of customer's needs.							
8. All of our business functions (e.g., marketing/sales, manufacturing, R&D, finance/accounting) are integrated in serving the needs of our target markets.							
9. Our business strategies are driven by our beliefs about how we can create greater value for our customers.							
10. We measure customer satisfaction systematically and frequently.							
11. We give close attention to after sales service.							
12. Top management regularly discusses competitors' strengths and strategies.							
13. All of our managers understand how everyone in our business can contribute to creating customer value.							
14. We target customers where we have an opportunity for competitive advantage.							
15. We share resources with other business units.							

long-run profits, it must continuously create superior value to its target customers. To create superior value for customers, a business should be customer oriented, competitor oriented, and interfunctionally oriented.[7]

A few years later after the first publications of Jaworski and Kohli, and Narver and Slater,[8] Deshpande, Farley, and Webster presented a different and new approach to market orientation concept.[9] In their study, they examined the impact of culture, customer orientation, and innovativeness on business performance. They have stressed that their method will contribute to the marketing field as follows:

1. "It is the first empirical study to relate simultaneously the concepts of organizational culture, customer orientation, and innovativeness to business performance.
2. It demonstrates a unique sampling and analytical method that involves carefully matched dyad pairs (called "quadrads") of manufacturers and their key customers.
3. It extends our emerging knowledge of customer orientation to non-US firms, specifically to large Japanese businesses on which much current scholarly and practitioner interest has been focused."[10]

In this study, they preferred the term "customer orientation" instead of "market orientation." In other words, they see customer and market Orientations as being synonymous.

They have prepared the original questionnaire in this study. The original questionnaire was prepared in English and translated into Japanese by a Japanese–American language instructor. The Japanese questionnaire was back translated by the research staff of a major Japanese university and modified for meaning. Customer orientation scale has been developed by them on the basis of extensive qualitative personal interviewing, a detailed survey of available literature, and pretesting in a small sample of firms. This is the third market orientation scale.[11]

Deshpande and Farley studied on to compare and retest the scales of three separate groups of researchers who developed measurements of a company's market orientation in the early 1990s.[12] They have examined three different scales measuring market orientation, which were developed more or less independently almost at the same time. In this study,

Table 7.3. Deshpande, Farley, and Webster Scale of Market Orientation

Scale Items	Strongly disagree	Disagree	Neither agree nor disagree	Agree	Strongly agree
We have routine or regular measures of customer service.	1	2	3	4	5
Our product or service development is based on good market and customer information.	1	2	3	4	5
We know our competitors well.	1	2	3	4	5
We have a good sense of how our customers value our products and services.	1	2	3	4	5
We are more customer focused than our competitors.	1	2	3	4	5
We compete primarily based on product or service differentiation.	1	2	3	4	5
The customer's interest should always come first, ahead of the owners.	1	2	3	4	5
Our products/services are the best in the business.	1	2	3	4	5
I believe this business exists primarily to serve customers.	1	2	3	4	5

they assessed the reliability of three scales in a dozen of international applications to see if the measurement procedures are reliable in different cultural settings—industrialized and industrializing, Asia and Europe, for example. Overall, the three scales of market orientation, while more or less independently, show remarkable similarity in terms of reliability and internal and external validity in this test using a multifirm, multinational sample of 82 marketing executives from 27 firms which are members of the Marketing Science Institute.[13] At the end of the study, Deshpande and Farley have defined market orientation as "the set of cross-functional processes and activities directed at creating and satisfying customers through continuous needs-assessment."

Matsuno, Mentzer, and Rentz compared these three market orientation scales and have developed an integrated model called the extended market orientation (EMO) model.[14]

The model in a way tries to combine several views and research results thus positioning organizational culture as one of several internal antecedents to conduct (i.e., market orientation as a set of behaviors). The authors

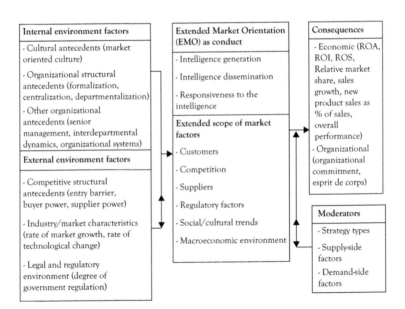

Figure 7.1. The extended market orientation conceptual model.
Source: Adapted from Matsuno, Mentzer, and Rentz (2005).[15]

have also added the environmental antecedents, internal or external, to the market orientation. They concluded that "Simultaneously, the breadth of market participants (e.g., competitors and customers) must be captured in the context of a firm's managerial actions. The general conceptual model of EMO and its focal EMO construct accommodates these two requirements. Specifically, the EMO scale extends the scope of stakeholders and marketplace factors to include suppliers, regulatory aspects, social and cultural trends and macroeconomic environment as other authors acknowledge."[16]

Chapter Summary

Different market orientation scales have been developed by different researchers. The measurement of market orientation is important because a company can learn its position in terms of market orientation, and by this way it can make necessary changes in its strategies. If we consider the empirical research results in the literature, being market oriented or not may play a vital role in the company's strategy as well as organization structure and organization culture.

In the marketing literature, there are three important scales which are used for measuring market orientation. These scales are commonly tested in marketing literature and considered to be are valid and reliable. These scales can be a guide for practical applications for companies. These scales are (1) MARKOR (a measure of market orientation), scale developed by Kohli, Jaworski, and Kumar in 1993.[17] (2) MKTOR, a scale developed by Narver and Slater in 1990.[18] (3) The third scale was developed by Deshpande, Farley, and Webster in 1993.[19]

MARKOR (a measure of market orientation) is one of very early scales developed to measure market orientation. This scale is a refined version of Jaworski and Kohli's scale (1990),[20] and was published in 1993 by Kohli, Jaworski, and Kumar, and named as MARKOR. The key features of this scale are (1) an expanded focus on market intelligence rather than customer intelligence; (2) an emphasis on a specific form of interfunctional coordination with respect to market intelligence; (3) a focus on activities related to intelligence processing rather than on the effect of these activities.

The second scale was developed by Narver and Slater which is a 15-item factor-weighted scale. In this study, Narver and Slater hypothesized that market orientation is a one-dimensional construct consisting of three behavioral components and two decision criteria: (1) customer orientation, (2) competitor orientation, (3) interfunctional coordination, (4) long-term focus, and a (5) profit objective.[21]

Deshpande, Farley, and Webster presented a different and new approach to market orientation concept.[22] In their study, they examined the impact of culture, customer orientation, and innovativeness on business performance. In this study, they preferred the term "customer orientation" instead of "market orientation." In other words, they see customer and market orientations as being synonymous. Deshpande, Farley, and Webster have prepared the original questionnaire in this study. Customer orientation scale has been developed by them on the basis of extensive qualitative personal interviewing, a detailed survey of available literature, and pretesting in a small sample of firms. This is the third market orientation scale.[23]

Matsuno et al. compared these three market orientation scales and have developed an integrated model called the EMO model.[24]

CHAPTER 8

Consequences of Market Orientation Effect on Organizational Performance

In this chapter, we will explain some important consequences of market orientation. Organizational performance, firm innovativeness, learning orientation, customer loyalty, and employees will be investigated as consequences of market orientation.

A Company Case

Cisco Customer Focus

Cisco has established a truly customer-focused culture throughout the organization and not just in the customer-facing departments. Everyone at Cisco is empowered to act on behalf of customers and acknowledge that we all have a role that impacts their behaviors and attitudes. Experts with years of industry knowledge and Internet business solutions experience bring high return on investments to our customers by understanding their perception of our products and services and their value. At Cisco, partnership is a key component of our strategy for delivering more complete and customized solutions to our customers. Through partnerships Cisco can offer complete networked-enabled productivity solutions that drive customer success today and in the future. We encourage our partners to use customer satisfaction knowledge to manage their businesses and improve our customer experience. Cisco promotes an environment where customer's opportunities are constantly analyzed and maximized by implementing business practices and methodologies that increase loyalty, satisfaction and retain customers' business over their lifetimes. Customers drive our business

(Continued)

(Continued)

strategies to achieving success and excellence in everything we do, and will continue to be our key focus for developing products and services that accelerate their capability to prosper in the Internet business.

Source: http://www.cisco.com/web/about/ac50/ac208/about_cisco _approach_to_quality_customer_success.html

As stated by Jaworski and Kohli, a market orientation is frequently posited to improve business performance. The argument is that organizations that are market-oriented, that is, those that track and respond to customer needs, and preferences can better satisfy customers and, hence, perform at higher levels.[1]

Many studies have examined the relationship between market orientation and business performance.[2] It is widely accepted that market orientation has a positive effect on business performance.[3] The relationship not only has been established firmly for large companies but also has been found in research on small medium-sized enterprises.[4]

Kirca, Jayachandran, and Bearden have found that market orientation has a positive impact on organizational performance.[5] This conclusion is consistent with several studies in the market orientation literature.[6]

A market orientation is likely to lead to improved performance because it is the organizational culture and climate that most effectively encourages the behaviors necessary for the creation of superior value for buyers and, therefore, continuous superior profit for the business.[7]

Jandaghi, Mokhles, and Pirani stated that "Organizational performance is the performance of an organization in financial and nonfinancial areas. In fact, any operation happens in an organization to improve or destroy the organization impacts on individuals' insights. It is true on market orientation. Customers expect organizational performance improvement in financial and nonfinancial areas if they feel that the rate of market orientation and attention to customer or rival as well as organizational accountability are all enhanced."[8]

The literature suggests that market orientation has primarily been a long-term focus but in relation to profits and in implementing each of the three behavioral components of market orientation.[9] Slater and Narver have hypothesized that market orientation is a one-dimensional construct consisting of three behavioral components and two decisions criteria are closely related. These authors stated that to create continuous superior value for customers, a business must be customer oriented, competitive oriented, and interfunctionally coordinated. They found that "for both the commodity and noncommodity business, market orientation is an important determinant profitability.

Among the noncommodity businesses the positive relationship between market orientation and a business's profitability appears to be monotonic, whereas among the commodity businesses a positive market orientation/profitability relationship is found only among businesses that are above the median in Market Orientation."[10]

According to Deshpande, a market orientation is likely to lead to improved performance because it is the organizational culture and climate that most effectively encourages the behaviors necessary for the creation of superior value for buyers and, therefore, continuous superior profit for the business.[11] Verhees and Meulenberg have found that there is a positive impact of market orientation on business performance;[12] customer market intelligence is positively related to the performance of small firms. All of these authors' research is related with small firms (Verhees and Meulenberg, p. 147).

Kumar et al. (2011) have examined two specific questions. These questions are as follows:[13]

1. Does market orientation create a source of sustainable competitive advantage, or is it a requirement that companies face when competing in today's business environment?
2. How much is gained, and how long can firms expect the advantages from developing a market orientation to hold?

According to the research results of Kumar et al. in comparing the main effect of market orientation on business performance, "Market orientation has a greater influence on profit than sales in both short and the long run. The carry over effect of market orientation of profit is greater than the effect of market orientation on sales."[14] They have stressed that having a market orientation makes organizations focus more on retention than acquisition, and therefore profits increase much more than sales. Kumar et al. also commented that "the adoption of a market orientation is important in generating both sales and profit. Given that the benefits of market orientation take time to become fully realized, the importance of top management in both emphasizing and supporting a market-oriented culture is paramount."[15]

The relationship between market orientation and corporate success has been examined by Fritz and Mundorf. These authors have stressed that the importance of market orientation for corporate leadership success is relatively great particularly under the following conditions:[16]

- Close cooperation among the departments of marketing, production, and R&D.
- Limited owner control, that is, high management control.
- Sales market as the main bottleneck to be overcome.
- Within consumer goods industry to a higher degree than within industrial goods sector.
- Considerable delegation of decision-making to lower levels of hierarchy.
- High cost of market entry for potential competitors.
- A very dynamic macroeconomic environment.

Effect on Firm Innovativeness

Intense competition, rapid globalization, and changing technology have made innovation as a must for firms. It is crucial for commercial organizations not only to capture new opportunities but also to pay more attention on the development of their products and market to maintain their competitive advantage.[17] Innovation has been defined by Jaskyte as "Implementation of an idea, service, process, procedure, system, structure, or product that is new to the prevailing organizational practice."[18] So an innovation implies change, but not all changes necessarily introduce new ideas or lead to significant improvements. Innovations can range from small incremental improvements, such as netbook computers, or radical breakthroughs, such as Toyota's battery-powered Prius car, observes Jaskyte.[19] What are the sources of innovation? In the literature, structural variables have been studied as potential sources of innovation. A comprehensive review of the structure–innovation relationship leads to the following consequences: First, organic structures positively influence innovation. Because they are lower in vertical differentiation, formalization, and centralization, organic organizations make the adoption of innovations easier. Second, long tenure in management is associated with innovation. Managerial tenure apparently provides legitimacy and knowledge of how to accomplish tasks and obtain desired outcomes. Third, innovation is nurtured when there are slack resources. Having an abundance of resources allows an organization to afford to purchase innovations, bear the cost of institution them, and absorb failures. Finally, interunit communication is high in innovative organizations.[20]

The innovation focus in marketing literature has been relatively product intensive. But market orientation is not related with not only product improvements but also with facilitating the social structure in an organization. This requires studying innovation on a broader scope while making the distinction between technologies-related versus social structure–related innovations.[21] Understanding of innovation requires an understanding based on four dimensions. These dimensions have been proposed by Henard and Szymanki.[22]
These are as follows:

1. Innovation in product
2. Strategy
3. Processes
4. Markets.

They stressed that technical aspects are enclosed in product, strategy, processes, and market innovations.

However, according to Atuahene-Gima (1996) "one of the most controversial recent debates in the literature concerns whether market orientation fosters innovation or leads to incremental developments in product portfolios derived from modifications in customer preferences."[23] The question raised is whether the most market-oriented firms tend to develop products with a higher degree of incorporated novelty or whether, if with an excessive customer orientation and short-term vision, they mainly focus on applying slight modifications to their product portfolio, in order to adapt it slowly to the changes detected in the market. Similarly, explicit acknowledgment of the positive effects that innovation has on entrepreneurial results[24] makes it desirable for market orientation to produce an effect on the firm's innovation activity, in terms of both the quantity and novelty of the new products developed. Han, Kim, and Srivastava found that the extent to which organizational innovations vary with market orientation depends on the level of technological turbulence and market turbulence.[25] Specifically, the authors found that customer orientation, competitor orientation, and interfunctional coordination facilitate technological and administrative innovations when technological turbulence is high. However, when market turbulence is high, only interfunctional coordination was found to have a positive effect.

Richard, Womack, and Allaway have the following five recommendations for companies that want to achieve innovative firm orientation.[26]

1. Take a generic view of your industry/firm. Determine how an industry/ firm has been defined and consider a broader definition. A firm's statement of corporate mission can help a firm define itself by examining the needs satisfied, lines of business it is engaged in, products sold, and so on.

2. Monitor other industries. In this area, Richard et al. stated that "you should be aware of marketing strategies in a wide range of industries. These industries can serve as sources of innovative strategies for satisfying existing consumers as well as attracting new consumers." In addition to these, these authors have stressed the importance of scanning business publications, as well as attending seminars.

3. Engage in benchmarking to determine the objectives for relevant areas of marketing. Once you have determined the objectives, you can develop a list of firms to emulate. Analyzing innovative strategies of the benchmark firms can help possible adaptation.

4. Recruit marketing people. Richard et al. observed that "marketing managers hired away from other industries can bring new perspectives and solutions to marketing problems. In essence, these people can be "debriefed" when added to the management team. In addition,

brainstorming sessions between these new and existing managers can yield new strategies."[27]

5. Be flexible enough to apply unique solutions to problems and change unsuccessful strategies. Management must encourage marketing managers to try new strategies without the fear of being reprimanded.

Hurley and Hult have introduced two innovation constructs into models of market orientation.[28]

1. The first one is innovativeness. Innovativeness is the notion of openness to new ideas as an aspect of a firm's culture. Innovativeness of the culture is a measure of the organization's orientation toward innovation.
2. The second one is the capacity to innovative. The capacity to innovative is a concept that was introduced by Burns and Stalker.[29] The capacity to innovative is the ability of the organization to adopt to implement new ideas, processes, or products successfully.[30]

To remain competitive and survive in the 21st century, companies can combine the marketing concept and cross-fertilization of ideas for innovative strategies.[31]

Traditionally, market orientation literature identifies positive relationships between market orientation and innovation. According to Küster and Vila (2011), market orientation behavior leads to more innovation and greater success with new products.[32] The relationship between market orientation and product innovation was investigated by Lukas and Ferrell.[33] Extant research has demonstrated a strong relationship between market orientation and innovativeness.[34]

According to Dibrell, Craig, and Hansen, market-oriented companies develop an in-depth understanding of manifest and latent needs of their customer base as well actions of competitors and often attempt to satisfy these desires through innovative products or services.[35] Hurley and Hult further recommended the inclusion of innovations in the market orientation concept.[36]

A positive relationship between market orientation and innovation strategy was also investigated by Küster and Vila.[37] According to their results, more market-oriented firms have a positive predisposition to innovate and this predisposition can help firms to increase their success. In addition to this, Küster and Vila have stressed that innovation decisions such as product innovation, strategy innovation, process innovation, and market innovation affect business success.[38]

Market orientation leads to incremental new product developments, and this is argued to be rationale for innovation that has the potential to create markets and customers. These researches[39] have suggested that innovation orientation mediates the relationship between market orientation and organizational performance.

As stated by Day, customer value and innovation benefit the firm when they are transformed into customer and brand assets. Another imperative is to capitalize on the customer as an asset. This requires selecting and developing loyal customers, protecting them from competitive attacks, and leveraging the asset beyond the core business. Strong brands attract and retain customers and thus need to be explicitly managed. The last imperative is to capitalize on the brand as an asset. This means strengthening the brand with coherent investments, protecting it against dilution and erosion, and then leveraging it fully to capture new opportunities.[40]

Effects on Employees

Kohli and Jaworski have stressed the importance of influence of market orientation on employees.[41] These authors have stated that these affects are not addressed in the extant literature. They suggested that a market orientation affords a number of psychological and social benefits to employees. They have stated that "several respondents noted that a market orientation leads to a sense of pride in belonging to an organization in which all departments and individuals work toward the common goal of serving customer. Accomplishing this objective results in employees sharing a feeling of worthwhile contribution, as well as higher levels of job satisfaction and commitment to the organization."[42]

According to Wei and Morgan, firms' training, hiring, and reward and evaluation systems should identify and should facilitate practices that enhance employee feelings of peer and manager supportiveness in order to enhance market orientation.[43] These authors have suggested some implementation. These are as follows. Specific suggestions for how this could be accomplished may include the following:

1. consideration of the empathetic and social interaction characteristics of potential employees in hiring decisions;
2. encouragement of informal and social interactions between managers and employees;
3. sensitivity training for all personnel; and
4. the identification, evaluation, and rewarding of management and employee behaviors that demonstrate supportiveness for fellow employees.[44]

As stated by Dursun and Kilic, having a workforce with a strong market orientation is especially important for a firm in the selling context.[45] These authors have noted that "if a firm is market oriented, it is more likely to take a planned action to train its sales employees to make them more market oriented. Since a marketer has a significant impact on the creating demand and establishing trust between the organization and the customer, the actions and behavior of a marketer and his/her orientation towards the customer become very significant and central from the organizational standpoint. If an organization aims to establish and/or maintain a competitive position in the marketplace and to develop long-term satisfactory relationships with its customers, it should definitely emphasize on understanding the factors that influence the customer oriented of its marketers."[46]

Webster has stressed that "employee morale is a critical success factor in the customer-oriented company, especially for employees who deliver some aspect of a product's service bundle. Management issues a clear statement of the value proposition, which becomes the focal point for the organization and a rallying cry for employees. It becomes part of the symbols and rituals of the organizational culture."[47]

Many executives have noted that a market orientation provides a number of psychological and social benefits to employees. In addition, a market orientation leads to a sense of pride in belonging to an organization in which all departments and individuals work toward the common goal of serving customers. These matters result in employees sharing a feeling of worthwhile contribution and stronger feelings of job satisfaction and commitment to the organization.[48]

Chapter Summary

Market orientation has some important outputs. In this chapter, we discussed the effects of market orientation on organizational performance, firm innovativeness, and employees. One of the most important consequences of market orientation is organizational performance. Many studies have examined the relationship between market orientation and business performance.

Intense competition, rapid globalization, and changing technology have made innovation a must for firms. It is crucial for commercial organizations not only to capture new opportunities but also to pay more attention on the development of their products and market to maintain their competitive advantage. Market orientation leads to new product developments, and this is argued to be rationale for innovation that has the potential to create markets and customers.

Many researchers have stressed that a market orientation has an influence on employees. According to Wei and Morgan, companies' training, hiring, and reward and evaluation systems should identify and facilitate practices that enhance employee feelings of peer and manager supportiveness in order to enhance market orientation.[49] These authors have suggested some implementation. Specific suggestions for how this could be accomplished may include the following: (1) consideration of the empathetic and social interaction characteristics of potential employees in hiring decisions, (2) encouragement of informal and social interactions between managers and employees, (3) sensitivity training for all personnel; and (4) the identification, evaluation, and rewarding of management and employee behaviors that demonstrate supportiveness for fellow employees.

CHAPTER 9

Market Orientation in International Markets

In Chapter 8, we discussed the consequences of market orientation. In this context, the effect of market orientation on organizational performance, firm innovativeness, and employees were explained. In this chapter, we will look at market orientation in international markets. Export market orientation will be explained. Additionally, we will look at the relationship between market orientation and niche marketing. The relationship between market orientation and information technology will also be examined in this chapter.

A Company Case

FXCM Recognized Again as Top Broker by Traders in the US

Investment Trends' April 2012 United States Foreign Exchange Report Names FXCM Number One in Overall Client Satisfaction, Online Education Materials, and Forex Provider

NEW YORK—(BUSINESS WIRE)—July 17, 2012–FXCM US (www.fxcm.com) has been recognized as the number one forex broker in several categories by the global market research group Investment Trends in their April 2012 United States Foreign Exchange Report. The awards were given for overall client satisfaction, education materials as well as being ranked the largest forex provider in the United States.*

Official FXCM Awards from Investment Trends United States Foreign Exchange Report:

- Number One in Overall Client Satisfaction
- Number One in Online Education Materials
- Largest Forex Provider

(*Continued*)

(*Continued*)

"We are extremely pleased to have been named number one forex broker for client satisfaction, education, and provider categories," said Drew Niv, FXCM CEO. Niv added, "We are constantly striving to provide our customers with the best service so that we can cater to all of their needs as a forex broker. Additionally, winning these awards shows us that we are meeting client expectations and we would like to thank our loyal clients for their continued support over the years."

The report's results came from a survey conducted in March and April 2012 with thousands of retail traders and investors in the United States participating. It is the largest known study of online retail investors in the United States.** The report found that in the US alone 120,000 individual investors traded forex at least once between April 2011 and April 2012. Additional findings within the study concluded that word of mouth recommendations are an important factor in choosing a broker and retail trader satisfaction in the US is extremely high.

Overall, FXCM has won awards worldwide from Investment Trends over the past year with repeated wins for "Best Education Materials and Programs" in the United States, United Kingdom, Australia, Germany, and France. "Overall client satisfaction" was another category in which FXCM excelled, being named a top broker in the United States, Germany, and France. "Being named a top winner in these categories outside of the United States shows that our efforts are consistent across all regions," said Sameer Bhopale, CMO of FXCM. "It is wonderful feedback from our customers, no matter where they are located, who are using our services. We are top ranked in education materials and client satisfaction categories."

Source: http://ir.fxcm.com/phoenix.zhtml?c=238885&p=irol-news Article_Print&ID=1715282&highlight=

One of the early studies of Dalgic may be considered as the first academic publication linking market orientation (MO) to international marketing field.[1] As observed by Dalgic "Despite the comparatively large volume of literature on market orientation in the domestic markets and large volume on international marketing activities, the relationship between market orientation and international marketing companies has not been investigated."[2]

Determining the construct of market orientation in international marketing is important. Dalgic hypothesized the following market orientation characteristics in international marketing by providing literature support:[3]

- "The greater the ability of a firm to generate organization-wide market intelligence, the greater the organization's ability to become market oriented in international marketing.
- The greater the firm's ability to disseminate market intelligence/information across departments, the greater the market orientation of the organization in international markets.
- The greater the organization's responsiveness to market intelligence/information, the greater the market orientation of the organization."[4]

The following adaptations have been suggested by Breman and Dalgic as an interpretation of national market orientation in an international marketing context. These authors have recommended replacing national market with international markets:

- Extraversion in international markets
- Organizational holism toward international marketing
- Responsiveness to international markets
- Long-term focus on international marketing
- Profit focus on in international marketing
- Relation focus in international marketing.

According to Breman and Dalgic, in order to apply international market orientation construct properly, a company must have some characteristics.[5] These characteristics are as follows:[6]

- Organization culture for international marketing
- Availability of an international marketing information system
- Flexibility of organization structures and roles of individuals
- Customer training
- Internal marketing
- Commitment to customer satisfaction thorough quality of goods and services.

Export Market Orientation

As stated by Cadogan, Diamantopoulos, and Siguaw, research on the subject of a firm's market orientation in its export operations is still in an early stage of development. Their definition of market orientation in export markets is as follows:[7]

1. the generation of market intelligence pertinent to the firm's exporting operations;
2. the dissemination of this information to appropriate decision makers;
3. the design and implementation of responses directed toward export customers, export competitors, and other extraneous export market factor which affect the firm and its ability to provide superior value for export customers.[8]

Cadogan and Diamantopoulos in an earlier qualitative study explored the meaning of market orientation in an export context.[9] In this context, Diamantopoulos and Cadogan's in-depth interviews uncovered particular items capturing some of the specificities of an export setting.[10] These authors found that the interactions of export personnel with nonexport personnel are critical in conducting effective market-oriented activities. In 1999, Cadogan, Diamantopoulos, and Mortanges developed an instrument to capture the degree to which firms exhibit market-oriented behaviors in their export operations. Using this scale, they then demonstrated that there were positive bivariate correlation coefficient between firms' levels of export market orientation activity and aspects of export performance. Cadogan, Diamantopoulos, and Mortanges have conceptualized the dimensions of export market orientation.[11]

- Export intelligence generation
- Export intelligence dissemination
- Export intelligence responsiveness
- Coordinating mechanism

Export market orientation can be conceived as a dynamic capability, which when associated with organizational learning, reinforces the managers' commitment to the internationalization process and so increases the level of financial, human, and managerial resources the managers dedicate to exporting.[12]

Cadogan et al.'s study presents a framework in which export market orientation activities export specific antecedents, export performance consequences, and the latter's potential moderating factors are modeled. They have focused on three key export-related variables as antecedents of export MO. These antecedents are as follows:[13]

- Export experience
- Export dependence
- Export coordination.

Export market orientation studies suggest that a well-developed export market orientation is associated with superior export performance.[14]

Market Orientation and Niche Marketing

Dalgic and Leeuw do give a series of steps/practical guidelines for the application of an overall niche strategy, which requires a market orientation application.[15] Here are the main points of niche marketing guidelines. As we can see, Steps 2–4 are closely related with market orientation:

- Step 1. Know yourself
- Step 2. Know your customer
- Step 3. Know your competitors
- Step 4. Develop a continuous information system
- Step 5. Apply differentiation
- Step 6. Do not compete in the same market segments with yourself
- Step 7. Create your safe haven
- Step 8. Do not spread too thin
- Step 9. Develop a corporate marketing strategy
- Step 10. Be alert: Be in control
- Step 11. Do not be static: look for new pastures continuously
- Step 12. Minimize your dependence on any one customer or product (pp. 52–53)

Niche marketing as an application of market orientation has been hailed as a successful strategy which can be attributed as a defensive or offensive strategy depending upon the market conditions. In the marketing literature several researchers studied the niche marketing principles. Table 9.1 summarizes the research recommendations for implementing a niche marketing strategy.

Table 9.1. Summary of Recommendations for Implementing Niche Marketing Strategies

Authors	Recommendations
Simon (1996) in Dalgic (2006) Ed.	Become an ultraspecialist • Follow a niche strategy—define markets very narrowly and create your own market • Cultivate strong mutual interdependence between you and your customer, built on economics and rationality (this helps to create strong entry barriers). • Match internal competencies with external opportunities. • Integrate technological orientation with marketing orientation. • Avoid outsourcing core activities.
Oviatt, B. M. & P.P. McDougal (1994) in Dalgic (2006) Ed.	Become a Global Player • Control (rather than own) assets particularly unique knowledge that create value in more than one country. • Importance of alternative governance structure to promote increased concentration of limited resources on the primary sources of competitive advantage. • Choose a product mix with demand that is of a global nature. • Maintain a global vision from inception. • Recruit internationally experienced managers with strong networks. • Sell a unique product with "pre-emptive" product attributes. • Maintain unique intangible assets such as tacit know-how to sustain advantage. • Maintain a program of incremental innovation.
McKinsey (1993) in Dalgic (2006) Ed. (7), Shani and Chalasani (1992)	Maintain a Strong Customer Orientation • Change with your customer. • Compete for value rather than price. • Strong customer focus and customize products to meet market requirements.
Dalgic (2006)	Be a Vocal Local • Differentiate based on local culture/lifestyle, products/services. • Establish a local identity. • Market through public relations and publicity.

Source: Adapted from Hamlin, Henry, and Cuthbert.[16]

Dalgic (2006) stressed the importance of market orientation in niche marketing practices: "Niche marketing could be viewed as the implementation of the marketing, in that niche marketing requires a customer/market-oriented organization which is customer focused, competitor oriented, responsive, anticipative, and functions in balance with the market and with internal resources, in pursuit of long-term relationships and sustainable profitability. Niche marketing is a continuous process."[17]

Dalgic classified some international companies as "strong customer-oriented niches" in the international marketing field. These company characteristics are derived from an industry survey.[18]

Strong customer-oriented niche characteristics include the following:

- As the customers change, they change.
- They compete on value through quality, technology, and product design.
- Cost competitiveness is important but it is a given factor.
- They have strong customer orientation and tailor products to meet customer requirements (this is more important than being technologically the best).
- They have a rich diversity of management skills, including skills in product and process innovation.
- The worldwide shift to smaller, more flexible manufacturing and a fall in the cost of communications and transport have been key factors in their growth.[19]

Relationship Between Information Technology and Market Orientation

New technologies and their applications have opened up new possibilities and opportunities for implementing market orientation. As Day suggested, information technology (IT) has a fundamental role in enabling organizations to develop new capabilities and skills that otherwise would be impossible to accomplish.[20] An integrated IT encompasses several elements: high-speed communication networks, facilitating a closer relationship with customers and commercial transactions through the Web; shared databases, disseminating information through an easily accessed repository; decision support systems, aiding managers to respond to the market; automatic product identification and tracking, crossing such information with purchasing patterns and developing customized offerings; balanced scorecard, monitoring company goals.

According to Prasad, Ramamurthy, and Naidu, the Internet and its collaborative environment allow organizations:[21]

1. an ease access to information on customers and competitors;
2. to share creative ideas from various sources (customers, suppliers, and partners), independently from the barriers of distance, language and time; and
3. a greater speed and flexibility in responding to customer needs.

As a conclusion, the Internet has become vital for gathering information on customer buying behaviors, competitors, environmental changes, for sharing information and knowledge, and for developing market-oriented responses, plans, and strategies by providing essential data.

According to the studies of Overby, Bharadwaj, and Sambamurthy and Min, Song, and Keebler,[22,23] IT strategic utilization—mainly Internet-based technologies and e-commerce—can positively influence market orientation by supporting the marketing activities. Though the sustainability of market orientation depends on values and norms, IT strategic use can enhance the firm's market orientation behaviors.[24]

The same authors observed that the operational definitions of business strategy rely on strategic orientation of business enterprise (STROBE) construct, and the IT strategy construct relies on the strategic orientation of information systems (STROIS) research instrument from Sabherwal and Chan, which segments Information Systems (IS) according to their functions, and investigates how well each one of these IS categories support business strategy.[25,26] For market orientation, the study adopts the classical model and instrument developed by Kohli and Jaworski with the contributions provided by Matsuno and Mentzer.[27,28] A meta-analysis study by Cano et al. points out that Kohli and Jaworski's instrument outperforms others, because their model explains more variance in the relationship between market orientation and business performance.[29] According to these operational definitions, a research protocol directs the

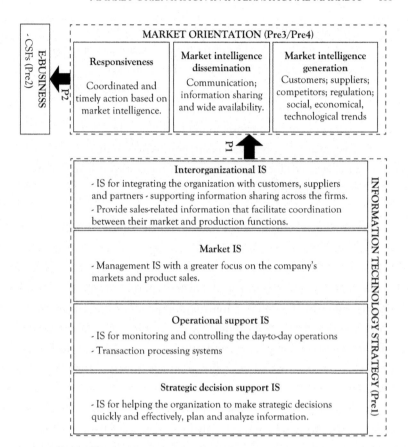

Figure 9.1. Market orientation and e-business relationship.
Source: Adapted from Borges, Hoppen, and Luce (2009).[31]

field research. The assessment of both IS categories and market orientation relies on a three-point scale: high (strong), medium, and low.[30]

Figure 9.1 explains these relationships. This framework represents e-business strategy as part of business strategy, either as just one more channel (click-and-mortar) or as a core business (dot-com).

Chapter Summary

In this chapter, we discussed market orientation in international markets. Determining the construct of market orientation in international marketing is important. Dalgic hypothesized the following market orientation characteristics in international marketing by providing literature support:[32]

- "The greater the ability of a firm to generate organization-wide market intelligence, the greater the organization's ability to become market oriented in international marketing.
- The greater the firm's ability to disseminate market intelligence/information across departments, the greater the market orientation of the organization in international markets.
- The greater the organization's responsiveness to market intelligence/information, the greater the market orientation of the organization."

As stated by Cadogan et al., research on the subject of a firm's MO in its export operations is still in an early stage of development.[33] Their definition of MO in export markets is as follows: (a) The generation of market intelligence pertinent to the firm's exporting operations, (b) the dissemination of this information to appropriate decision makers, and (c) the design and implementation of responses directed toward export customers, export competitors, and other extraneous export market factor that affect the firm and its ability to provide superior value for export customers.

Niche marketing as an application of MO has been hailed as a successful strategy, which can be attributed as a defensive or offensive strategy depending upon the market conditions. In the marketing literature, several researchers studied the niche marketing principles.

New technologies and their applications have opened up new possibilities and opportunities for implementing MO. As Day suggested IT has a fundamental role in enabling organizations to develop new capabilities, and skills that otherwise would be impossible to accomplish. An integrated IT encompasses several elements: high-speed communication networks, facilitating a closer relationship with customers and commercial transactions through the Web; shared databases, disseminating information through an easily accessed repository; decision support systems, aiding managers to respond to the market; automatic product identification and tracking, crossing such information with purchasing patterns and developing customized offerings; balanced scorecard, monitoring company goals.[34]

Notes

Introduction

1. Dalgic (1994).

Chapter 1

1. Berkowitz, Kerin, and Rudelius (1989).
2. Ferrell and Hartline (2011), p. 51.
3. Keith (1960).
4. Keith (1960), p. 36.
5. Kotler and Armstrong (2012), p. 9.
6. Fullerton (1988), p. 108.
7. Mooradian, Matzler, Ring (2012), p. 154.
8. Ford (1922), p. 72.
9. Kotler (1998).
10. Miller and Layton (2001).
11. Kotler and Armstrong (2012).
12. Kotler and Armstrong (2012), p. 10.
13. Mullins and Walker (2010), p. 38.
14. McCarthy and Perreault, (1987), p. 27.
15. Keith (1960).
16. Kotler and Armstrong (2012).
17. Lindgren and Shimp (1996), p. 18.
18. Lamb, Hair, and McDaniel (2011), p. 4.
19. Webster (1988).
20. Kotler and Keller (2012), p.18.
21. Ferrell and Hartline (2011), p. 51.
22. Mooradian, Matzler, and Ring (2012), p. 3.
23. Hise (1965).
24. Houston (1986).
25. O'Leary and Iredale (1976), p. 146.
26. Houston (1986), p. 85.
27. Drucker (1954), p. 37.
28. Verghis (2006), p. 17.
29. Dibb et al. (1991), p. 13.
30. Carl and Gates (1998).
31. Carl and Gates (1998).
32. Kotler and Armstrong (2012).

33. Kotler and Armstrong (2012), p. 10.
34. Lamb, Hair, and McDaniel (2011).
35. Kerin, Hartley, and Rudelius (2011).
36. Mooraidan, Matzler, and Ring (2012), p. 155.
37. Kotler and Keller (2012).
38. Mooraidan, Matzler, and Ring (2012), p. 156.
39. Hawkins, Best, and Coney (1998), p. 377.
40. Hawkins, Best and Coney (1998), p. 378.
41. Peter and Donnelly (1998).
42. Pride and Ferrel (1989).
43. Paul and Donnelly (1991).
44. King (1991).
45. Lamb, Hair, and McDaniel (2011), pp. 7–11.
46. McCarthy and Perreault (1987), p. 31.
47. Slater and Narver (1994a).
48. Slater and Narver (1994a), p. 47.
49. Heiens (2000).
50. Heiens (2000).
51. Deshpande, Farley, and Webster (1993).
52. Deshpande, Farley, and Webster (1993).
53. Slater and Narver (1994b), p. 23.
54. Heiens (2000).
55. Heiens (2000).
56. Kohli and Jaworski (1990), p. 13.
57. Heiens (2000).
58. Hult (2011), p. 1.
59. Lavidge (1970), p. 27.
60. Kotler and Armstrong (2012), p. 11.
61. Lindgren and Shimp (1996), p. 24.
62. Kotler and Armstrong (2012), p. 11.
63. Lamb, Hair, and McDaniel (2011), p. 6.

Chapter 2

1. Ruekert (1992), p. 225.
2. Shapiro (1988); Webster (1988); Kohli and Jaworski (1990).
3. Kohli and Jaworski (1990).
4. Kobylanski and Szulc (2011), p. 51.
5. Schlosser and McNaughton (2004).
6. Zollo and Winter (2002).
7. Schlosser and McNaughton (2004), p. 13.

8. Kohli and Jaworski (1990); Narver and Slater (1990); Jaworski and Kohli (1993); Gima (1995); Greenlay (1995).

9. Deshpande, Farley, and Webster (1993); Cavusgil and Zou (1994); Pelham (1997); Pulendran, Speed, and Widing (2000); Liu, Xeuming, and Yi-Zheng (2003); Deshpande and Farley (2004).

10. Dalgic (2000), p. 20.

11. Zebal (2003).

12. Johnson (1998).

13. Johnson (1998), p. 8.

14. Shapiro (1988), p. 120.

15. Shapiro (1988) p. 122.

16. Kohli and Jaworski (1990).

17. Kohli, Jaworski, and Kumar (1993).

18. Narver and Slater (1990).

19. Day (1994).

20. Deshpande et al. (1993).

21. Narver and Slater (1990).

22. Slater and Narver (1994b).

23. Webster (1988), p. 37.

24. Cravens (1997), p. 7.

25. Ruekert (1992), p. 228.

26. Zebal (2003), p. 40.

27. Ruekert (1992).

28. Lafferty and Hult (2001).

29. Lafferty and Hult (2001), p. 95.

30. Levitt (1960) pp. 45–56.

31. Levitt (1960) p. 50.

32. Levitt (1960) p. 47.

33. Kotler and Keller (2012), p. 7.

34. Richard, Womack, and Allaway (1992).

35. Richard et al. (1992), p. 67.

36. Solomon (2012), p. 175.

37. Richard et al. (1992), p. 67.

38. Kotler (1988).

39. Bennett (2005), p. 392.

40. Richard et al. (1992), p. 68.

41. Richard et al. (1992), p. 68.

42. Richard et al. (1992), p. 69.

43. Smith, Drumwright, and Gentile (2009).

44. Gonzalez-Padron, Hult, and Isabelle (2010), pp. 93–96.

45. Gonzalez-Padron et al. (2010), p. 95.

46. Gonzalez-Padron et al. (2010).
47. Wei-Skillern (2004).
48. Dalgic (2000), p. 20.

Chapter 3

1. Manu (1992).
2. Grönroos (1994).
3. Grönroos (1994); Piercy (1985, 1992); Webster (1988).
4. Grönroos (1991).
5. Grönroos (1997), p. 329.
6. Sheth, Gardner, and Garrett (1988) p. 195.
7. Grönroos (1991).
8. Berry (1983), p. 25.
9. Harker (1999), p. 16.
10. Sin et al. (2005).
11. Reichheld (2001).
12. McKenna (1991), pp. 65–79.
13. Büschke (2004).
14. Keiningham, et al. (2005).
15. Gordon (2005), p. 47.
16. Madhavan, Shah, and Grover (1994a).
17. Schlesinger and Heskett (1991).
18. Schlesinger and Heskett (1991).
19. Reichheld (1996).
20. Dalgic (1998).
21. Copulsky and Wolf (1990).
22. Treacy and Wiersema (1993).
23. Shaw (1991).
24. Parasuraman, Zeithaml, and Berry (1985, 1988).
25. Grönroos (1994).
26. Dalgic (1998).

Chapter 4

1. Felton (1959); King (1965); Barksdale and Darden (1971); Day (1994).
2. Harris and Ogbonna (2000), p. 318.
3. Craven (1997).
4. Day (1994).
5. Day (1994).
6. Day (1994), p. 41.
7. Day (1994).

8. Day (1994), p. 41.
9. Webster (1994).
10. Webster (1994), p. 10.
11. Webster (1994), p. 11.
12. Dibrell, Craig, and Hansen (2011), p. 469.
13. Webster (1994), p. 11.
14. Webster (1994), p. 11.
15. Kotler and Keller (2012), p. 231.
16. Webster (1994), p. 11.
17. Webster (1994) p. 12.
18. Day (1994), p. 48.
19. Treacy and Wiersema (1993).
20. Lindgren and Shimp (1996), p. 250.
21. Garvin (1987).
22. Schonberger (1990), p. 52.
23. Kok, Hillebrand, and Biemans (2003).
24. Ferrell and Hartline (2011), p. 371.
25. Webster (1994).
26. Webster (1994), p. 13.
27. Zeithlam (1981).
28. Kotler and Keller (2012), p. 140.
29. Webster (1994), p. 13.
30. Kerin, Hartley, and Rudelius (2011), pp. 250–251.
31. Kerin, Hartley, and Rudelius (2011) p. 251.
32. Kerin, Hartley, and Rudelius (2011) p. 251.
33. Drucker (1989).
34. Webster, Malter, and Ganesan (2005), p. 36.
35. Webster (1988).
36. Breman and Dalgic (2000).
37. Slater and Narver (1994), p. 23.
38. Craven (1997), p. 8.
39. Breman and Dalgic (2000).
40. Day (1994).
41. Day (1994), p. 48.
42. Day (1994), p. 48.
43. Craven (1997), p. 9.
44. Ferrel and Hartline (2011).
45. Ferrel and Hartline (2011), p. 53.
46. Deshpande, Farley, and Webster (1993); Narver and Slater (1990); Jaworski and Kohli (1993).
47. Graves and Matsuno (2004).
48. Graves and Matsuno (2004).

49. Webster (1995).
50. Menon et al. (1999); Bigne et al. (2000); Morgan and Strong (1998); Piercy (1998).
51. Tokarczyk et al. (2007)
52. Hurley and Hult (1998); Kohli and Jaworski (1990); Narver and Slater, (1990); Slater and Narver (1998, 1999).
53. Kumar, Subramanian, and Yauger (1998).
54. Tokarczyk et al. (2007).
55. Hunt and Lambe (2000).
56. Hunt and Morgan (1995).
57. Tokarczyk et al. (2007).
58. Kumar et al. (1998).
59. Dobni and Luffman (2000).
60. Menon et al. (1999).
61. Bourgeois and Eisenhardt (1988); Kohli and Jaworski (1990).
62. Deshpande et al. (1993), pp. 23–27.
63. Robbins and Judge (2011), p. 520.
64. Cameron and Freeman (1991).
65. Quinn (1988).
66. Simberova (2009); Deshpande et al. (1993).
67. Simberova (2009), p. 517.
68. Desphande et al. (1993), p. 26.
69. Cameron and Freeman (1991); Simberova (2009), p. 517.
70. Desphande et al. (1993), p. 26.
71. Webster (1994).
72. Gebhardt, Carpenter, and Sherry (2006), p. 42.
73. Kilman, Saxton, and Serpa (1985).
74. Schein (1992).
75. Deshpande and Webster (1989), p. 4.
76. Schein (1984).
77. Hatch (1993).
78. Trice and Beyer (1993).
79. Schein (1992); Trice and Beyer (1993).
80. Hatch (1993).
81. Hatch (1993), p. 660.
82. Yoon and Lee (2005).
83. Yoon and Lee (2005), p. 3.
84. Homburg and Pflesser (2000).
85. Homburg and Pflesser (2000), p. 451.
86. Homburg and Pflesser (2000), p. 451.
87. Slater and Narver (1994).

88. Slater and Narver (1994), p. 26.
89. Slater and Narver (1994), p. 26.
90. Webster (1994).

Chapter 5

1. Kohli and Jaworski (1990); Kelly (1992); Ruekert (1992); Jaworski and Kohli (1993); Wood and Bhuian (1993); Gounaris and Avlonitis (1997); Harris(1999); Cervera, Molla, and Sanchez (2001).

2. Narver and Slater (1990); Deshpande, Farley, and Webster (1993); Jaworski and Kohli (1993); Siguaw, Brown, and Widing (1994).

3. Kohli and Jaworski (1990).

4. Felton (1959); Levitt (1969); Webster (1988); Kohli and Jaworski (1990).

5. Pulendran, Speed, and Widing (2000), p. 124.

6. Jaworski and Kohli (1993), p. 55.

7. Deshpande(1999), p. 107.

8. Felton (1959), p. 55.

9. Felton (1959), p. 55.

10. Kohli and Jaworski (1990), p. 7.

11. Levitt (1969), p. 244.

12. Craven (1997), p. 9.

13. Webster (1988).

14. Webster (1988), p. 37.

15. Webster (1988).

16. Tomaskova(2009).

17. Tomaskova(2009), p. 539.

18. Jaworski and Kohli (1993); Zebal (2003).

19. Kumar et al. (2011), p. 16.

20. Payne (1988).

21. Jaworski and Kohli (1993).

22. Jaworski and Kohli (1993).

23. Slater and Narver (1994b).

24. Pulendran et al. (2000).

25. Kirca, Jayachandran, and Bearden (2005), p. 37.

26. Robbins and Judge (2011), p. 182.

27. Deshpande and Webster (1989); Kohli and Jaworski (1990); Jaworski and Kohli (1993); Wood and Bhuian (1993).

28. Wood and Bhuian (1993).

29. Jaworski and Kohli (1993).

30. Kohli and Jaworski (1990).

31. Jaworski and Kohli (1993).

32. Jaworski and Kohli (1993), p. 64.
33. Bennet and O'Brien (1994).
34. Han, Kim, and Srivastava (1998).
35. Dalgic (2000).
36. Kohli and Jaworski (1990), p. 10.
37. Kohli and Jaworski (1990); Jaworski and Kohli (1993); Deshpande (1999).
38. Anderson and Chambers (1985); Jaworski (1988); Kohli and Jaworski (1990); Jaworski and Kohli (1993); Sigauw, Brown, and Widing (1994); Pulendran et al. (2000).
39. Hetherington (1991).
40. Hall, Haas, and Johnson (1967).
41. Robbins and Judge (2011), p. 493.
42. Aiken and Hage (1968).
43. Robbins and Judge (2011).
44. Jaworski and Kohli (1993).
45. Harris (2000).
46. Jaworski and Kohli (1990).
47. Robbins and Judge (2011).
48. Anderson and Chambers (1985); Kohli and Jaworski (1990); Pulendran et al. (2000).
49. Webster (1988), p. 38.
50. Jaworski and Kohli (1993), p. 56.
51. Dalgic (2000), p. 31.
52. Sigauw et al. (1994).
53. Pulendran et al. (2000), p. 127.
54. Porter, Allen, and Angel (1981).
55. Kohli and Jaworski (1990), p. 12.
56. Harris and Piercy (1999).
57. Kohli and Jaworski (1990).
58. Dutton and Walton (1966); Kohli and Jaworski (1990); Jaworski and Kohli (1993).
59. Levitt (1969).
60. Dutton and Walton (1966).
61. Dalgic (2000), p. 31.
62. Deshpande (1999), p. 10.
63. Jaworski and Kohli (1993).
64. Kohli and Jaworski (1990).
65. Kennedy, Goolsby, and Arnould (2003).
66. Deshpande (1999), p. 10.
67. Lawrence and Lorsch (1967); Deshpande and Zaltman (1982); Jaworski and Kohli (1993).
68. Jaworski and Kohli (1993).

69. Deshpande and Zaltman (1982).
70. Kohli and Jaworski (1990).
71. Kohli and Jaworski (1990), p. 15.
72. Kohli and Jaworski (1990).

Chapter 6

1. Dalgic (2000), p. 33.
2. Dalgic (2000), p. 34.
3. Dalgic (2000).
4. Dalgic (2000), p. 35.
5. Gebhardt, Carpenter, and Sherry (2009).
6. Edwards (2005).
7. Gebhardt et al. (2009).
8. Gebhardt et al. (2009).
9. Gebhardt et al. (2009). http://insight.kellogg.northwestern.edu/index.php
   /Kellogg/article/walking_the_walk
10. Narver, Slater, and Tietje (1998).
11. Kotter's (1995).
12. Payne (1988).
13. Swartz (1990).
14. Lear (1963).
15. Lear (1963), p. 59.
16. Masiello (1988), p. 86.
17. Webster (1988), p. 29.
18. Webster (1988), p. 37.
19. Mullins and Walker (2010), p. 37.
20. Mullins and Walker (2010), p. 39.
21. Dalgic (2000).
22. Slater and Narver (1995).
23. Dalgic (2000).
24. Arndt (1979).
25. Dalgic (2000), p. 29.
26. Dalgic (2000).
27. Gebhardt et al. (2009).
28. Dalgic (2000).

Chapter 7

1. Kohli, Jaworski, and Kumar (1993).
2. Narver and Slater (1990).
3. Deshpande, Farley, and Webster (1993).

4. Jaworski and Kohli (1990).
5. Kohli et al. (1993), p. 468.
6. Narver and Slater (1990).
7. Narver and Slater (1990), p. 22.
8. Jaworski and Kohli (1990); Narver and Slater (1990).
9. Deshpande et al. (1993).
10. Deshpande et al. (1993), p. 24.
11. Deshpande et al. (1993).
12. Deshpande and Farley (1998).
13. Deshpande and Farley (1998), p. 225.
14. Matsuno, Mentzer, and Rentz (2003).
15. Matsuno Mentzer, and Rentz (2005), p. 3.
16. Matsuno et al. (2005), p. 4.
17. Kohli et al. 1993.
18. Narver and Slater (1990).
19. Deshpande et al. (1993).
20. Jaworski and Kohli (1990).
21. Narver and Slater (1990).
22. Deshpande et al. (1993).
23. Deshpande et al. (1993).
24. Matsuno et al. (2003).

Chapter 8

1. Jaworski and Kohli (1993), p. 48.
2. Narver and Slater (1990); Jaworski and Kohli (1993); Slater and Narver (1994); Kirca, Jayachandran, and Bearden (2005); Jandaghi, Mokhles, and Pirani (2011); Kumar et al. (2011).
3. Narver and Slater (1990); Jaworski and Kohli (1993); Desphande (1999).
4. Verhees and Meulenberg (2004).
5. Kirca et al. (2005).
6. Narver and Slater (1990); Jaworski and Kohli (1993).
7. Deshpande (1999), pp. 111–112.
8. Jandaghi et al. (2011), p. 4.
9. Houston (1986); Kohli and Jaworski (1990); Slater and Narver (1990).
10. Slater and Narver (1990), p. 32.
11. Deshpande (1999), pp. 111–112.
12. Verhees and Meulenberg (2004).
13. Kumar et al. (2011), p. 16.
14. Kumar et al. (2011).
15. Kumar et al. (2011), p. 28.

16. Fritz and Mundorf (1994), p. 17.
17. Maatoofi and Tajeddini (2011), p. 20.
18. Jaskyte (2005).
19. Jaskyte (2005).
20. Robbins and Judge (2011) p. 604.
21. Han, Kim, and Srivastava (1998).
22. Henard and Szymanki (2001).
23. Atuahene-Gima (1996).
24. Han et al. (1998).
25. Han et al. (1998).
26. Richard, Womack, and Allaway (1992), p. 70.
27. Richard et al. (1992), p. 70.
28. Hurley and Hult (1998).
29. Burns and Stalker (1961).
30. Hurley and Hult (1998) p. 44.
31. Richard et al. (1992), p. 70.
32. Küster and Vila (2011), p. 40.
33. Lukas and Ferrell (2000).
34. Deshpande, Farley, and Webster (1993); Han et al. (1998); Hurley and Hult (1998); Kirca et al. (2005); Dibrell, Craig, and Hansen (2011); Küster and Vila (2011).
35. Dibrell et al. (2011), p. 469.
36. Hurley and Hult (1998).
37. Küster and Vila (2011).
38. Küster and Vila (2011), p. 48.
39. Deshpande et al. (1993); Desphande and Farley (2004).
40. Day (2011), p. 186.
41. Kohli and Jaworski (1990).
42. Kohli and Jaworski (1990), p. 13.
43. Wei and Morgan (2004), p. 385.
44. Wei and Morgan (2004), p. 385.
45. Dursun and Kilic (2011).
46. Dursun and Kilic (2011), p. 55.
47. Webster (1994), p. 28.
48. Desphande (1999), p. 33.
49. Wei and Morgan (2004).

Chapter 9

1. Diamantopoulos and Cadogan (1996), pp. 24–25.
2. Dalgic (1994), p. 69.

3. Dalgic (1994).

4. Dalgic (1994), pp. 75–78.

5. Breman and Dalgic (2000).

6. Breman and Dalgic (2000), p. 345.

7. Cadogan, Diamantopoulos, and Siguaw (2002).

8. Cadogan, Diamantopoulos, and Siguaw (2002), p. 616.

9. Cadogan and Diamantopoulos (1995).

10. Diamantopoulos and Cadogan (1996).

11. Cadogan, Diamantopoulos, and Mortanges (1999).

12. Navarro et al. (2011), p. 189.

13. Cadogan et al. (2002).

14. Cadogan et al. (2001); Cadogan et al. (2002).

15. Dalgic and Leeuw (1994), pp. 52–53.

16. Hamlin, Henry, and Cuthbert, (2012), p. 32.

17. Dalgic (2006), p. 22.

18. Dalgic (2006).

19. McKinsey (1993).

20. Day (1994).

21. Prasad, Ramamurthy, and Naidu (2001).

22. Overby, Bharadwaj, and Sambamurthy (2006).

23. Min, Song, and Keebler (2002).

24. Borges, Hoppen, and Luce (2009).

25. Venkatraman (1989).

26. Sabherwal and Chan (2001).

27. Kohli and Jaworski (1990).

28. Matsuno and Mentzer (2000).

29. Cano et al. (2004).

30. Borges, Hoppen, and Luce (2009).

31. Borges et al. (2009), p. 886.

32. Dalgic (1994).

33. Cadogan et al. (2002).

34. Day (1994).

References

Aiken, M., & Hage, J. (1968). Organizational independence and intra-organizational structure. *American Sociological Review 33*, 912–930.

Anderson, P., & Chambers, T. (1985). A reward measurement model of organizational buying behaviour. *Journal of Marketing 49*(2), 7–23.

Arndt, J. (1979). Toward a concept of domesticated market. *Journal of Marketing 43*(Fall), 69–75.

Atuahene-Gima, K. (1996). Market orientation and innovation. *Journal of Business Research 35*(2), 93–103.

Barksdale, C. H., & Darden, B. (1971). Marketers' attitudes toward the marketing concept. *Journal of Marketing 35*, 29–36

Bennet, J. K., & O'Brien, M. J. (1994). The building blocks of the learning organisation. *Training* 41–49.

Bennett, R. (2005). Factors encouraging competitive myopia in the performing arts sector: an empirical investigation. *The Service Industries Journal 25*(3), 391–401.

Berkowitz, N. E., Kerin, A. R., & Rudelius, W. (1989). *Marketing.* Homewood, IL: Irwin.

Berry, L. L. (1983). Relationship marketing. In L. L. Berry, G. L. Shostack, and G. D. Upah, (Eds.), *Emerging perspectives of services marketing.* Chicago, IL: American Marketing Association.

Borges, M., Hoppen, N., & Luce, B. F. (2009). Information technology impact on market orientation in e-business. *Journal of Business Research 62*(9), 883–890.

Bradley, F. (2003). *Strategic marketing in the consumer driven organization.* West Sussex, New York: John Wiley & Sons Inc.

Breman, P., & Dalgic, T. (2000). Market orientation and learning organization: the case of Dutch exporting firms. *Advances in International Marketing 10*, 339–387.

Buchanan, R., & Gilles, C. (1990). Value managed relationship: the key to customer retention and profitability. *European Management Journal 8*(4), 523–526.

Büschken, J. (2004). *Higher profits through customer lock-in.* New York: Thomson .

Cadogan, W. J., & Diamantopoulos, A. (1995). Narver and Slater, Kohli and Jaworski and the market orientation construct: integration and internationalization. *Journal of Strategic Marketing 3*(1), 41–60.

Cadogan, W. J., Diamantopoulos, A., & de Mortanges C. P. (1999). A measure of export market orientation: scale development and cross-cultural validation. *Journal of International Business Studies 30*(4), 689–707.

Cadogan, W. J., Diamantopoulos, A., & Siguaw, A. J. (2002). Export market oriented activities: their antecedents and performance sequences. *Journal of International Business Studies 33*(3), 615–626.

Cameron, S. K., & Freeman, J. S. (1991). Cultural congruence, strength and type: relationship to effectiveness. *Research in Organizational Change and Development 5*, 23–58.

Carl, M., & Gates, R. (1998). *Marketing research essentials* (2nd ed.). Ohio: South-Western College Publishing.

Cavusgil, T., & Shaoming Z. (1994). Marketing strategy and performance relationship: an investigation of the empirical link in export market ventures. *Journal of Marketing 58*, 1–21.

Cervera, A., Molla, A., & Sanchez, M. (2001). Antecedents and consequences of market orientation in public organizations. *European Journal of Marketing 35*(11/12), 1259–1286.

Copulsky, R. J., & Wolf, J. M. (1990). Relationship marketing: positioning for the future. *Journal of Business Strategy 11*(4), 16–20.

Craven, W. D. (1997). *Strategic marketing* (5th ed.). Homewood: Irwin.

Dalgic, T. (1994). Market orientation and international marketing: a conceptual attempt at integration. *Advances in International Marketing 6*(6), 69–82.

Dalgic, T. (1998). Niche marketing principles-Guerrillas vs. Gorillas. *Journal of Segmentation in Marketing 2*(1), 5–18.

Dalgic, T. (2000). Market orientation and its implementation. In: B. Keith (Ed.), *The Oxford Textbook of marketing* (pp. 20–37). Oxford: Oxford University Press.

Dalgic, T. (2006). *Handbook of niche marketing principles and practice*. New York: The Haworth Reference Press.

Dalgic, T., & Leeuw, M. (1994). Niche marketing revisited: concept, applications and some European cases. *European Journal of Marketing 28*(4), 39–55.

Day, S. G. (1994). The capabilities of market-driven organizations. *Journal of Marketing 58*(4), 37–52.

Day, S. G. (2011). Closing the marketing capabilities gap. *Journal of Marketing 75*(4), 183–195.

Day, S. G., & Wensley, R. (1988). Assessing advantage: a framework for diagnosing competitive superiority. *Journal of Marketing 52*, 1–20.

Deshpande, R. (1999). *Developing Market Orientation*. Sage Publications. Deshpande, R., & Farley, J. U. (1998). Measuring market orientation: generalization and synthesis. *Journal of Market Focused Management 2*(3), 213–232.

Deshpande, R., & Farley J. U.. (2004). Organizational culture, market orientation, innovativeness and firm performance: an international research odyssey. *International Journal of Research in Marketing 21*(1), 3–23.

Deshpande, R., Farley, J. U., & Webster E. F. (1993). Corporate culture, customer orientation, and innovativeness in Japanese firms. A quadrad analysis. *Journal of Marketing 57*(1), 23–27.

Deshpande, R., & Webster, Jr. F. E. (1989). Organizational culture and marketing: defining the research agenda. *Journal of Marketing*, *53*(1), 3–15.

Deshpande, R., & Zaltman, G. (1982). Factors affecting the use of market research information: a path analysis. *Journal of Marketing*, *19*, 14–31.

Diamantopoulos, A., & Cadogan, W. J. (1996). Internationalizing the market orientation construct: an in-depth interview approach. *Journal of Strategic Marketing 4*(1), 23–52.

Dibb, S., Simkin, L. P., Pride, M., William, F. O. C. (1991). *Marketing: concepts and strategies, European edition*. Houghton Mifflin Company.

Dibrell, C., Craig, J., & Hansen, E. (2011). Natural environment, market orientation, and firm innovativeness: an organizational life cycle perspective. *Journal of Small Business Management 49*(3), 467–489.

Drucker, P. (1954). *The practice of management*. Harper & Row: New York.

Dursun, T., & Kilic, C. (2011). Exploring occupational and strategic drivers of individual customer orientation. *Journal of Business and Economics Research 9*(5), 55–66.

Dutton, J. M., & Walton, R. E. (1966). Interdepartmental conflict and cooperation: two contrasting studies. *Human Organization 25*(4), 207–220.

Edwards, C. (2005). Shaking up Intel's insides. *Business Week 3918*, 35.

Felton, A. P. (1959). Making the marketing concept work. *Harvard Business Review 37*, 55–65.

Ferrell, O. C., Gonzalez-Padron, T. L., Hult, G. T. M., & Maignan, I. (2010). From market orientation to stakeholder orientation. *Journal of Public Policy and Marketing 29*(1), 93–96.

Ferrell, O. C., & Hartline D. M. (2011). *Marketing strategy* (5th ed.). South-Western Cengage Learning.

Ford H. (1922). *My life and work*. New York: Garden City Publishing Co. Inc.

Fritz, W., & Mundorf, N. (1994). Market orientation and corporate success: findings from Germany. Available from http://www.wiwi.tubs.de/marketing/publikationen/ap/download/AP94-13.pdf

Fullerton, R. A. (1988). How modern is modern marketing? Marketing's evolution and the myth of the production era. *Journal of Marketing 52*(1), 108–125.

Garvin, D. (1987). Competing on the eight dimensions of quality. *Harvard Business Review 65*, 202–209.

Gebhardt, F., Carpenter, G., Gregory, S., & Sherry, Jr. J. F. (2006). Creating a market orientation: a longitudinal, multifirm, grounded analysis of cultural transformation. *Journal of Marketing 70*, 37–55.

Gebhardt, G., Carpenter, G., & Sherry, F. J. (2009). Walking the walk: creating a market orientation. Available from http://insight.kellogg.northwestern.edu/index.php/Kellogg/article/walking_the_walk

Gordon, E. R. M. (2005). *Locking in loyalty* (Book Review). September/October.

Gounaris, S. P., & Avlonitis, G. J. (1997) Company and market correlates of marketing orientation development: an empirical investigation. *26 EMAC Conference*, Warwick, 20–23 May, pp. 536–555.

Graves, J. R., & Matsuno, K. Three research perspectives on market orientation. Retrieved April 2, 2012 from http://www.researchnest.com

Greenlay, E. G. (1995). Market orientation and company performance: empirical evidence from UK companies. *British Journal of Management 16*(1), 1–13.

Grönroos, C. (1994). From marketing mix to relationship marketing: towards a paradigm shift in marketing. *Management Decision 32*(2), 4–20.

Grönroos, C. (1997). Keynote paper from marketing mix to relationship marketing—towards a paradigm shift in marketing. *Management Decision*, *35*(4), 322–339.

Hall, H. R., Haas, E., & Johnson, J. N. (1967). Organizational size, complexity, and formalization. *American Sociological Review 32*, 901–911.

Hamlin, R., Henry, J., & Cuthbert, R. (2012). Acquiring market flexibility via niche portfolios: the case of Fisher & Paykel White Goods. Retrieved April 24, 2012, from http://otago.ourarchive.ac.nz/bitstream/handle/10523/2072/ejmflexibilityworkingpaper.pdf?sequence=1

Han, J. K., Kim, N., & Srivastava, R. (1998). Market orientation and organizational performance: is innovation a missing link? *Journal of Marketing 62*(4), 30–45.

Harker, M. J. (1999). Relationship marketing defined? An examination of current relationship marketing definitions. *Marketing Intelligence and Planning 17*(1), 13–20.

Harris, L. C. (1999). Barriers to developing market orientation. *Journal of Applied Management Studies 8*(1), 85–101.

Harris, L. C. (2000). The organizational barriers to developing market orientation. *European Journal of Marketing 34*(5/6), 598–624.

Harris, L. C., & Emmanuel, O. (2000). The responses of front-line employees to market oriented culture change. *European Journal of Marketing*, *34*(3/4), 318–340..

Harris, L. C., & Piercy, N. F. (1999). A contingency approach to market orientation: distinguishing behaviours, systems, structures, strategies and performance characteristics. *Journal of Marketing Management 15*, 617–646.

Hatch, Ja M. (1993). The dynamics of organizational culture. *The Academy of Management Review 18*(4), 657–693.

Hawkins, D. I, Best, R. J., & Cone, K. A. (1998). *Consumer behavior, building marketing strategy* (7th ed.). Boston: McGraw Hill.

Heiens, R. A. (2000). Market orientation: toward an integrated framework. *Academy of Marketing Science Review*. Retrieved May 1, 2012, from http://www.amsreview.org/amsrev/forum/heiens01-00.html

Henard, D. H., & Szymanski, D. M. (2001). Why some new products are more successful than others. *Journal of Marketing Research XXXVIII*, 362–375.

Hetherington, R. W. (1991). The effects of formalization on departments of a multi-hospital system. *Journal of Management Studies 28*(2), 103–140.

Hise, R. T. (1965). Have manufacturing firms adopted the marketing concept. *Journal of Marketing 29*, 9–12.

Homburg, C., & Pflesser, C. (2000). A multiple-layer of market-oriented organizational culture: measurement issues and performance outcomes. *Journal of Marketing Research XXXVII*, 449–462.

Houston, F. S. (1986). The marketing concept: what it is and what it is not. *Journal of Marketing 50*(2), 81–87.

Hult, T. (2011). Market-focused sustainability: market orientation plus! *Journal of the Academy of Marketing Science 39*, 1–6.

Hurley, R., & Hunt, T. (1998). Innovation, market orientation, and organizational learning: an integration and empirical examination. *Journal of Marketing 62*, 42–54.

Jandaghi, G., Mokhles, A., & Pirani, P. (2011). Studying the impacts of market orientation on clients' social value, conceived quality and loyalty as well as its mutual on the performance of Qom Hamrah-E-Avval Telecommunication company. *Business and Management Review 1*(7), 01–08.

Jaskyte, K. (2005). Organizational culture and innovation in nonprofit organizations. *Research Report II*. Retrieved April 22, 2012, from http://kjaskyte.myweb.uga.edu/NSFAnnualReport2.pdf

Jawoski, B. J., & Kohli, A. K. (1993). Market orientation: antecedents and consequences. *Journal of Marketing 57*(3), 53–70.

Johnson, M. D. (1998). *Customer orientation and market action*. Upper Saddle River, NJ: Prentice-Hall.

Keiningham, T. L., Vavra, T. G., Aksoy, L., & Wallard, H. (2005). *Loyalty myths*. Hoboken, NJ: John Wiley & Sons.

Keith, R. J. (1960). The marketing revolution. *Journal of Marketing 24*(1), 35–38.

Kennedy, K. N., Goolsby, J. R., & Arnould, E. J. (2003). Implementing a customer orientation: extension of theory and application. *Journal of Marketing, 67*, 67–81.

Kerin, R. A., Hartley, S. W., & Rudelius, W. (2011). *Marketing*. New York: McGraw-Hill Irwin.

Kilman, R. H., Saxton, M. J., & Serpa, R. (1985). Introduction: five key issues in understanding and changing culture. In R. H. Kilman, M. J. Saxton, R. Serpa & Associates (Eds.). *Gaining control of the corporate culture* (pp. 1–16). San Francisco, CA: Jossey-Bass.

King, R. L. (1991). The marketing concept: fact or intelligent platitude. In P. Paul & J. Donnelly (eds.) *A preface to marketing management* (5th ed.). Homewood, IL: Richard D. Irwin, Inc.

Kirca, H. A., Jayachandran, S., & Bearden, W. O. (2005). Market orientation: a meta-analytic review and assessment of its antecedents and impact on performance. *Journal of Marketing 69*, 24–41.

Kobylanski, A., & Szulc, R. (2011). Development of marketing orientation in small and medium-sized enterprises. Evidence from Eastern Europe. *International Journal of Management and Marketing Research 4*(1), 49–59.

Kohli, A. K., & Jawoski, B. J. (1990). Market orientation: the construct, research propositions, and managerial implications. *Journal of Marketing 54*(2), 1–18.

Kohli, A. K., Jawoski, B. J., & Kumar, A. (1993). MARKOR: a measure of market orientation. *Journal of Marketing Research XXX*, 467–477.

Kok, R. A. W., Hillebrand, B., & Biemans, W. G. (2003). What makes product development market oriented? Towards a conceptual framework. *International Journal of Innovation Management 7*(2), 137–162.

Kotler, P. (1998). *Marketing management.* Upper Saddle River: Prentice-Hall.

Kotter, J. P. (1995). Leading change: why transformation efforts fail. *Harvard Business Review 73*(2), 59–67.

Kotler, P., & Armstrong, G. (2012). *Principles of marketing* (14th ed.). Upper Saddle River: Prentice-Hall.

Kotler, P., & Keller, K. L. (2012). *Marketing management* (14th ed.). Upper Saddle River: Prentice-Hall.

Kumar, V., Jones, E., Venkatesan, R., & Leone, R. P. (2011). Is market orientation a source of sustainable competitive advantage or simply the cost of competing? *Journal of Marketing 75*(1), 16–30.

Küster, I., & Vila, N. (2011). The market orientation–innovation success relationship: the role of internationalization strategy. *Innovation Management, Policy and Practice 13*(1), 36–54.

Lafferty, B. A., & Hult, T. M. G. (2001). A synthesis of contemporary market orientation perspectives. *European Journal of Marketing 35*(1/2), 92–109.

Lamb, C., Hair Jr., J. F., & McDaniel, C. (2011). *Mktg 4.* South-Western Cengage Learning.

Lavidge, R. J. (1970). The growing responsibilities of marketing. *Journal of Marketing 34*, 25–28.

Lawrence, P. R., & Lorsch, J. W. (1967). Differentiation and integration in complex organizations. *Administrative Science Quarterly 12*(2), 1–47.

Lear, R. W. (1963). No easy road to market orientation. *Harvard Business Review 41*, 53–60.

Levitt, T. (1960). Marketing myopia. *Harvard Business Review 38*(4), 45–56.

Lindgren, J. H., & Shimp, T. A. (1996). *Marketing an interactive learning system,* Orlando: The Dryden Press Harcourt Brace College Publishers.

Liu S. S., Xeuming, L., & Yi-Zheng, S. (2003). Market oriented organization in an emerging economy: a study of missing links. *Journal of Business Research, 56*(6), 481–492.

Lukas, B. A., & Ferrell, O. C. (2000). The effect of market orientation on product innovation. *Journal of the Academy of Marketing Science, 28*(2), 239–247.

Maatoofi, A. R., & Tajeddini, K. (2011). Effect of market orientation and entrepreneurial orientation on innovation. *Journal of Management Research 11*, 20–30.

Madhavan, R., Shah, R. H., & Grover, R. (1994). Motivations for and theoretical foundations of relationship marketing. *AMA Winter Educator's Conference Proceedings*, St. Petersburg: American Marketing Association 19–21/02/1994, 183–190.

Manu, F. (1992). Innovation orientation, environment and performance: a comparison of US and European markets. *Journal of International Business Studies 2*, 333–359.

Masiello, T. (1988). Developing market responsiveness throughout your company. *Industrial Marketing Management 17*, 85–93.

Matsuno, K., Mentzer J. T., & Rentz, J. O. (2005). A conceptual and empirical comparison of three market orientation scales. *Journal of Business Research 58*(1), 1–8.

McCarthy, J. E., & Perreault, W. D. (1987). *Basic marketing* (9th ed.). Homewood: Irwin.

McKenna, R. (1991). Marketing is everything. *Harvard Business Review 69*(1), 65–79.

McKinsey and Company and Australian Manufacturing Council (1993). *Emerging exporters—Australia's high value added manufacturing exporters.* Melbourne: Australian Manufacturing Council.

Menon, A., Bharadwaj, S., Phani Tej, A., & Edison, S. (1999). Antecedents and consequences of marketing strategy making: a model and a test. *Journal of Marketing 63*(2), 18–40.

Miller, K. E., & Layton, R. A. (2001). *Fundamentals of marketing*, (4th ed.). Roseville, New South Wales: McGraw-Hill Book Company Australia Private Limited.

Min, S., Song, S., & Keebler, J. S. (2002). An internet-mediated market orientation (IMO): building a theory. *Journal of Marketing Theory and Practice 10*(2), 1–11.

Mooradian, T. A., Matzler, K., & Ring, L. J. (2012). *Strategic marketing.* Upper Saddle River: Prentice-Hall Pearson.

Mullins, J. W., & Walker, O. C. (2010). *Marketing management. A strategic decision making approach* (7th ed.). New York: McGraw-Hill/Irwin.

Narver, J. C., & Slater, S. F. (1990). The effect of a market orientation on business profitability. *Journal of Marketing 54*(4), 20–35.

Narver, J. C., & Slater, S. F., & Tietje, B. C. (1998). Creating a market orientation. *Journal of Market Focused Management 2*(1), 241–255.

Navarro, A., Acedo, F. J., Losada, F., & Ruzo, E. (2011). Integrated model of export activity: analysis of heterogeneity in managers' orientations and perceptions on strategic marketing management in foreign markets. *The Journal of Marketing Theory and Practice 19*(2), 187–204.

O'leary, R., & Iredale, I (1976). The marketing concept: quo vadis? *European Journal of Marketing, 10*(3), 146–157.

Overby, E., Bharadwaj, A., & Sambamurthy, V. (2006). Enterprise agility and the enabling role of information technology. *European Journal of Information Systems 15*, 120–131.

Parasuraman, A., Berry, L., & Zeithlam, V. (1988). SERVQUAL: a multiple item scale for measuring consumer perceptions on service quality. *Journal of Retailing 64*, 12–37.

Parasuraman, A., Zeithlam, V., & Berry, L. (1985). A conceptual model of service quality and its implications for future research. *Journal of Marketing 49*, 41–50.

Payne, A. F. (1988). Developing a marketing-oriented organization. *Business Horizons 31*(3), 46–53.

Pelham, A. (1997). Mediating influences on the relationship between market orientation and profitability in small industrial firms. *Journal of Marketing Theory and Practice 5*, 55–76.

Peter, J. J., & Donnelly, J. H. (1998). *Marketing management-knowledge and skills* (5th ed.). Boston, Mass.: Irwin, McGraw-Hill.

Piercy, N. (1985). *Marketing organization. An analysis of information processing, power and politics.* London: George Allen & Unwin.

Piercy, N. (1992). *Marketing-led strategic change.* Oxford: Butterworth Heinemann.

Porter, L. W., Allen, R. W., & Angel, H. (1981). The politics of upward influence in organizations. In B. Staw & L. Cummings (Eds), *Research in organizational behaviour, 3*, Greenwich, CT: JAI Press, Inc.

Prasad, V. K., Ramamurthy, K., & Naidu, G. M. (2001). The influence of internet-marketing integration on marketing competencies and export performance. *Journal of International Marketing 9*(4), 82–110.

Pride, W. M., & Ferrell, O. C. (1989). *Marketing: concepts and strategies* (6th ed.). Boston: Houghton Mifflin Co.

Pulendran, S., Speed, R., & Widing, R. E. (2000). The antecedents and consequences of market orientation in Australia. *Australian Journal of Management 25*(2), 119–143.

Quinn, R. E. (1988). *Beyond rational management: mastering the paradoxes and competing demands of high performance.* San Francisco, CA: Jossey-Bass.

Reichheld, F. (2001). *The loyalty effect.* Massachusetts: Harvard Business School Press.

Reichheld, F. F., & Sasser, W. (1990). Zero defects: quality comes to services. *Harvard Business Review, 68*(5), 105–111.

Richard, M. D., Womack, J. A., & Allaway, A. W. (1992). An integrated view of marketing myopia. *The Journal of Consumer Marketing 9*(3), 65–71.

Robbins, S. P., & Judge, T. A. (2011). *Organizational behavior* (14th ed.). Upper Saddle River: Prentice-Hall.

Ruekert, R. W. (1992). Developing a market orientation: an organizational strategy perspective. *International Journal of Research in Marketing 9*(3), 225–245.

Schein, E. H. (1985). How culture forms, develops and changes. In R. H. Kilman, M. J. Saxton, R. Serpa, and Associates (Eds.), *Gaining control of the corporate culture* (pp. 17–43). San Francisco, CA: Jossey-Bass.

Schlesinger, L., & Heskett, J. (1991). Breaking the cycle of failure in service. *Sloan Management Review 32*(3) Spring, 17–28.

Schlosser, F. K., & McNaughton, R. B. (2004). *Building competitive advantage upon market orientation: constructive criticisms and a strategic solution.* Quebec City, Quebec: ASAC.

Schonberger, R. J. (1990). *Building a chain of customers: linking business functions to create the world class company.* New York: Free Press.

Shapiro, B. P. (1988). What the hell is market oriented? *Harvard Business Review, 66*(6), 119–125.

Shaw, R. (1991). *Computer aided marketing & selling,* Oxford: Butterworth Heinemann.

Sheth, J. N., Gardner, D. M., & Garrett, D. E. (1988). Marketing theory: evolution and evaluation, New York: Wiley.

Siguaw, J. A., Brown, G., & Widing, R. E. (1994). The influence of market orientation of the firm on sales force behaviour and attitudes. *Journal of Marketing Research 31*(1), 106–116.

Simberova, I. (2009). Corporate culture as a barrier of market orientation implementation. *Economics and Management 14*, 513–521.

Sin, L. Y. M., Alan, T., Oliver, Y., Raymond, C., & Jenny, L. (2005). Market orientation, relationship marketing orientation, and business performance: the moderating effects of economic ideology and industry type. *Journal of International Marketing 13*(1), 36–57.

Slater, S. F., & Narver, J. C. (1994a). Does competitive environment moderate the market orientation-performance relationship? *Journal of Marketing 58*(1), 46–55.

Slater, S. F., & Narver, J. C. (1994b). Market orientation, customer value, and superior performance. *Business Horizons*, March–April, 22–28.

Slater, S. F., & Narver, J. C. (1995). Market orientation and the learning organization. *Journal of Marketing 59*, 63–74.

Smith, C., Drumwright, M. E., & Gentile, M. C. (2009). The new marketing myopia. Retrieved April 24, 2012, from http://papers.ssrn.com/sol3/papers.cfm?

Solomon K. A. (2012). The evolution of the marketing concepts: theoretically different roads leading to practically same destination. *Global Conference on Business and Finance Proceedings 7*(1), 173–183.

Swartz, G. (1990). Organizing to become market-driven. Conference summary. *Marketing Science Institute Conference* Report, Boston, Massachusetts, 90–123.

Tokarczyk, J., Hansen, E., Green, M., & Down, J. (2007). A resource-based view and market orientation theory examination of the role of "familiness" in family business success. *Family Business Review 20*(1), 17–31.

Tomaskova, E. (2009). Internal barriers of market orientation application. *Economics and Management 14*, 535–540.

Treacy, M., & Wiersema, F. (1993). Customer intimacy and other value disciplines. *Harvard Business Review*, January–February, 84–93.

Trice, H. M., & Beyer, J. M. (1993). *The cultures of work organizations*. Englewood Cliffs, NJ: Prentice-Hall.

Verghis, P. (2006). *The ultimate customer support executive unleash the power of your customer*. Summit: Silicon Press.

Verhees, F. J. H. M., Meulenberg, M. T. G. (2004). Market orientation, innovativeness, product innovation and performance in small firms. *Journal of Small Business Management 42*(2), 134–155.

Webster, F. E. (1988). The rediscovery of the marketing concept. *Business Horizons 31*(3), 29–39.

Webster, F. (1994). Executing the new marketing concept. *Marketing Management 3*(1), 8–16.

Webster, F., Malter, A. J., & Ganesan, S. (2005). The decline and dispersion of marketing competence. *MIT Sloan Management Review 46*(4), 35–43.

Wei, Y. S., & Morgan, A. N. (2004). Supportiveness of organizational climate, market orientation, and new product performance in Chinese firms. *Journal of Product Innovation Management 21*, 375–388.Wei-Skillern, J. (2004). The evolution of Shell's stakeholder approach—a case study. *Business Ethics Quarterly, 14*(4), 713–716.

Wood, W. R., & Bhuian, S. N. (1993). Market orientation and nonprofit organizations: performance associations and research propositions. *Journal of Nonprofit and Public Sector Marketing 1*(1), 7–32.

Yoon, S.-J., & Lee, S.-H. (2005). Market-oriented culture and strategy: are they synergistic? *Marketing Bulletin 16*, 1–20 . Retrieved from http://marketing bulletin.massey.ac.nz

Zebal, A. M. (2003). A synthesis model of market orientation for a developing country—the case of Bangladesh. PhD Thesis, Victoria University of Technology, Melbourne, Australia.

Zeithaml, V. A. (1981). How consumer evaluation processes differ between goods and services, In J. Donnelly & W. George (Eds.), *Marketing of services* (pp. 186–190). Chicago, IL: American Marketing Association.

Zollo, M., & Winter, G. S. (2002). Deliberate learning and the evolution of dynamic capabilities. *Organization Science 13*(3), 339–351.

Index

OTHER TITLES IN THE MARKETING STRATEGY COLLECTION

Naresh Malhotra, Georgia Tech, Collection Editor

- *Developing Winning Brand Strategies* by Lars Finskud
- *Conscious Branding* by David Funk and Anne Marie Levis
- *Marketing Strategy in Play: Questioning to Create Difference* by Mark Hill
- *Decision Equity: The Ultimate Metric to Connect Marketing Actions to Profits* by Piyush Kumar and Kunal Gupta
- *Building a Marketing Plan: A Complete Guide* by Ho Yin Wong, Roshnee Ramsaran-Fowdar, and Kylie Radel
- *Top Market Strategy: Applying the 80/20 Rule* by Elizabeth Kruger
- *Pricing Segmentation and Analytics* by Tudor Bodea and Mark Ferguson
- *Strategic Marketing: Planning for the Small to Medium Sized Business* by David Anderson
- *Expanding Customer Service as a Profit Center Striving for Excellence and Competitive Advantage* by Rob Reider
- *Applying Scientific Reasoning to the Field of Marketing Make Better Decisions* by Terry Grapentine

Announcing the Business Expert Press Digital Library
Concise E-books Business Students Need for Classroom and Research